ALTERNATING MASKS

ALTERNATING MASKS

*Selected Poems
of Kornelijus Platelis*

*Translated from the Lithuanian
by Jonas Zdanys*

Copyright © 2021 Jonas Zdanys, All Rights Reserved.

ISBN 978-1-7338882-7-1

Alternating Masks: Selected Poems of Kornelijus Platelis was published in Brooklyn, New York, on July 1, 2021, by Black Spruce Press.

The translation of this book was supported by the Lithuanian Culture Institute.

Acknowledgments
A number of these translations have appeared in the following books: *Two Voices/Du Balsai*. Jonas Zdanys and Kornelijus Platelis. *Poems and Translations*. (Chicago: Purple Flag Press, 2017); *Solitary Architectures: Selected Poems of Kornelijus Platelis*. Translated by Jonas Zdanys. (Beaumont: Lamar University Press 2014); *Kornelijus Platelis: Haiku*. Translated by Jonas Zdanys. (New Haven: Pierson College Press of Yale University 2007). Illustrated by Joanna Zdanys. *Zones: Poems by Kornelijus Platelis*. Translated by Jonas Zdanys and Kerry Shawn Keys. (Chicago: Virtual Artists Collective 2004); *@ and Other Poems* by Kornelijus Platelis. Translated by Jonas Zdanys and Kerry Shawn Keys. (Vilnius: Vario Burnos 2002). *Four Poets of Lithuania: Vytautas P. Bloze, Sigitas Geda, Nijolė Miliauskaitė, Kornelijus Platelis*. Selected and Translated by Jonas Zdanys. (Vilnius: Vaga Publishers Ltd. 1995).

blacksprucepress.org
blacksprucepress@gmail.com
Design by forgetgutenberg.com
Cover photograph © Algimantas Aleksandravičius

Manufactured in the United States of America

Contents

Introduction / i

I

From *Words and Days* (*Žodžiai ir dienos*, 1980)

The Carpet on the Wall / 1
Milk and Tomatoes / 2
The Runner / 3

From *Home on the Bridge* (*Namai ant tilto*, 1984)

An Encounter at Dusk / 5
Seaside Quartet / 6
Tiresias / 7
A Poem About Solitary Architecture / 8
Overtaken Fog / 9
The Glance / 10
Pastoral / 11
The Raven / 12
My Grandmother's History / 13
Restorers / 15
The Miracle of Wine / 17
The Wedding Procession / 19
The Way of Flax / 20

From *Snare for the Wind* (*Pinklės vėjui*, 1987)

Proteus / 22
Midday / 23
The Forests' Betrothed / 24
Breaking Glass / 25
Secret Conversations / 26
The Descending Swan / 27
Melancholy / 28

Confession / 29
A Quiet Evening / 30
The Cut / 31
Starlings / 32
Czech Etude / 33
Periplum / 35
Ghosts / 37
An Empty House / 39
Morning Concert / 40
Forest Duel / 42
While Sifting Through the Pile of Slag I Find a Beer Bottle Cap / 43
An Epic Poet in Spring / 44
War's Beginning / 45
Sunrise / 46
A Yotvingian's Prayer Riding to Fight the Enemy / 47
An Encounter in the Forest / 49
Triptych with a Laughing Woman / 51

From *The Boat Shell* (*Luoto kevalas*, 1990)

Country Morning / 55
Christmas in the Forest / 56
Intruders / 58
The Miracle of Blood / 59
Zone / 61
Civil Defense Instructions / 62
On the Other Side of the Glass / 63
For the Departing / 66
Raise High the Mast, Carpenters! / 67
The Girl and the Unicorn / 68
A Christmas Hymn / 69
The Start of Hunting Season / 72
Nihilists / 73
Gamblers / 74
Epiphanies / 75
Advice to the Adept / 76
Spider / 77

Two Ways / 78
Bookish Vengeance / 79
Ave, Caesar / 81
The Labyrinth / 83

II

From *Orations to the River* (*Prakalbos upei*, 1995)

Apocrypha / 89
Court Case / 90
The Jinn / 91
The Peaceable Song / 94

From *Tidal Zone* (*Atoslūgio juosta*, 2000)

About Starlings Ten Years Later / 98
Fisherman / 99
I Don't Worry About Culture / 100
Rodeo / 101
Tidal Zone / 102
The Top / 103
Home / 104
Night Bather / 105
Apples / 106
Hades Kidnaps Persephone / 107
Aging Gods / 108
St. Elizabeth's Hospital / 109
The Barbarian / 111
Suburban Pine Forests / 112
Unexpected Guests / 113
The Necessities of a Diary / 114
Evening Music / 115
Sunfish Heads / 116
The Fisher Hawk / 117
Nasturtium / 118

A View of the Sea / 119
Rolling / 122
Ode to a Cracked Vase / 123
Delayed in Ephesus / 124

III

From *Palimpsests* (*Palimpsestai*, 2004)

The Tiller of the Soil / 129
Waking in Silence / 130
An Ordinary Meeting / 131
Primavera / 132
Time to Write and Time to Change / 133
The Woman in Front of the Shop Window / 134
An Ordinary Ascent / 135
Campo de Fiori / 136
The Magi / 137
Passover / 138
Nobody / 140
Another Rendezvous / 142
Birdie / 144
Palimpsests / 145
A Cry in Sleep / 146
Spring in the Middle of Fall / 147
A Personal Carnival / 148
About Beautiful Women / 149
The Mermaid's Complaint / 150
The Fruit of Concord / 151
Fifty-Year-Old Women / 152
Clinical Observations / 153
Petaludes / 154
Aegean Wine / 155
Pyromaniacs / 156
Honor and Justice / 157
Copyright © / 158

From *Cave Phenomena* (*Karstiniai reiškiniai*, 2010)

Cave Phenomena / 160
About Gods and People / 162
A Shabby Dwelling / 163
A Discussion About Lions / 165
The Goddess of Oblivion / 166
Outlines / 167
About Starlings After Yet Another Five Years / 170
Portrait / 171
The Faceless / 172
Autumn's Flowers / 173
A Cookie for Persephone / 174
The Square / 175
Vita Nuova / 176
A Troubled Year / 177
Also Died / 178
Wanting to Be / 179
Speleologists / 181
I Met that Starling Later in Dublin / 182
Confrontation in the Museum / 183
The Transfigured Stairs / 184
The Followed / 185
Family History / 186
The Arrival Hall / 187
Don't Talk Loudly / 188
The Christmas Bird / 189
Haiku, Senryu, and Other Very Short Poems / 190

IV

From *Ruptured Moonlights* (*Įtrūkusios mėnesienos*, 2018)

A Partial Eclipse / 201
Golem's Crew / 202
The Passion According to Pilate / 203
Exodus / 204

February 28th / 205
Spring Readings / 206
On Both Sides / 207
One Spring / 208
Milk / 209
If I Wasn't a Poet, I'd Be / 210
Burning a Life / 211
Dust / 213
Cleaning the Cistern / 214
Swamp People / 215
The Ivory Tower / 216
Fragmentation: Phrygians / 217
The Difficulties of Integrating into Society / 218
The Prosecutor / 219
Stolen Cows / 220
Thimble Dance / 221
The Art of Love / 222
Satire in Winter / 227
The Poetess' Grave / 230
Anniversary / 231
Bicycles in the Garage / 232
Sixty-Year-Old Women / 233
July. Ikebana / 234
Safe Rendezvous / 235
The Carp / 236
Naiad / 237
A Strange Flower / 239
Dream Thief / 240
The Rose Tunic / 241
Monument / 243
Foxwoods Casino / 244
Journey's End / 245

From *Tarnishing Mirrors* (*Korijantys veidrodžiai*, 2021)

The Tarnishing Mirror / 246
Praying Mantis / 247
Metaphysics / 248

St. Jerome's Apologia / 250
Heavenship / 251
Showfee / 252
Toward Home / 253
Phantom of the Opera / 254
Mimesis / 255
The Tracked Down / 256
Field of Vision / 257
The Magic Flute / 258
The Tree of Knowledge / 259
Pythia / 260
Mermaid / 261
From CONVERSATIONS WITH LI PO *about mutually pleasant things*
    The Great Autumn Moon / 262
    Masks / 263
    The Temple on the Hill / 264
    In A Boat of Spice Wood / 265
    Shadow / 266
The Naturalist's Resurrection / 267
To Autumn / 268
The Sitters / 269
Swifts / 270
Bindweed / 271
The Sowers of Seeds / 272
The Wooden Duck / 273

About the Translator / 275

Introduction

Kornelijus Platelis was born in 1951 in Šiauliai, in north-central Lithuania. He graduated from the Vilnius Building Institute in 1973 and worked until 1988 as an engineer in Druskininkai, a resort town in southern Lithuania along the banks of the Nemunas River. He published his first poems in 1977 and is the author of ten collections of poetry: *Žodžiai ir dienos* (*Words and Days*, 1980), *Namai ant tilto* (*A Home on the Bridge*, 1984), *Pinklės vėjui* (*A Snare for the Wind*, 1987), *Luoto kevalas* (*The Boat Shell*, 1990), *Prakalbos upei* (*Orations to the River*, a volume of selected poems, 1995), *Atoslūgio juosta* (*Tidal Zone*, 2000), *Palimpsestai* (*Palimpsests*, 2004), *Karstiniai reiškiniai* (*Cave Phenomena*, 2010), *Įtrūkusios mėnesienos* (*Ruptured Moonlights*, 2018), and *Korijantys veidrodžiai* (*Tarnishing Mirrors*, 2021). His extended essay on the ecology of culture, *Būstas prie Nemuno* (*Being by the Nemunas*), was published in 1989, and his collection of essays on poetry, *Ir mes praeiname* (*And We Are Passing*), appeared in 2011. He has also translated many of the most important American and British poets into Lithuanian—among them John Keats, Ezra Pound, T.S. Eliot, e.e.cummings, Ted Hughes, and Seamus Heaney—and Polish poets Adam Mickiewicz, Czesław Miłosz, Adam Tadeusz Naruszewicz, and Wisława Szymborska. He was also instrumental in developing commentary for a new Lithuanian edition of the Bible. His work has been translated into Armenian, Belarusian, Chinese, Czech, English, Estonian, French, Gaelic, Galician, Georgian, German, Hungarian, Italian, Japanese, Korean, Latvian, Macedonian, Norwegian, Polish, Russian, Slovenian, Spanish, Swedish, and Ukrainian, and has appeared in various anthologies and editions throughout the world.

In 1988 Platelis joined the democratic liberation movement Sąjudis, and, after Lithuania reestablished its independence from the Soviet Union, he served in the administration of Vytautas Landsbergis as Vice Minister for Culture and Education and then as Minister of Education and Science in the administration of President Valdas Adamkus. He has also served as Deputy Mayor of Druskininkai, as Director of the Vaga Publishing House, and from 2001 until 2014 as Editor-in-Chief of *Literatūra ir menas* (*Literature and Art*), the leading Lithuanian literary and cultural journal. He has also served as President of the Lithuanian Association of Creative Artists, as a Member of the Board of National

i

Radio and Television, as Board member of the Fund for Press, Radio and Television, and as Chairman of the Board of the international annual literary festival "Druskininkai Poetic Fall." Among his many honors and awards is the Lithuanian National Award for Culture and Arts (2002) and fellowships and grants from Lithuanian and Scandinavian sources.

Platelis' poetry, as the work in this gathering of all the translations I have made of his poems illustrates, is a mixture of political and declarative styles on the one hand and mystical intensity, metaphysical questioning, and exploration of myth on the other. At its core is active affiliation with the sensibilities of a generation of writers who, as Platelis describes them in his essay "On the Civic Role of Poetry," were nihilists when they began their creative work, women and men with a violated system of values whose work is futuristic or hermetic and whose aesthetic sensibilities are motivated by a certain artistic and cultural rebellion that is itself the product of a "contradictory reality." The work of the poets of his generation, Platelis believes, constitutes the frame of the renaissance of contemporary Lithuanian poetry. Their poems are concerned with the ultimate search for beauty and with the hope of the possibility of realizing that goal, and they approach that search through poetic experimentation marked by aestheticism and light decadence, where artifice and complexity are guiding and foundational creative propositions.

Platelis' poetry, though, aims at a higher plane as well, one on which questions of personal and social ethics and the possibility of an ethical culture can be considered and resolved. In that effort, Platelis is concerned with the revivification of individual and cultural biography, in which there is a need to recognize and atone for the "faults / we gathered in the labyrinth of history." The process of that atonement, for Platelis, finds its most powerful resonance in the heroic dimensions of the human spirit—often presented through the guideposts of myth—and in their linkages to absolute moral values, which are tied as well to aesthetic and cultural principles. It is a theme he explores in *Būstas prie Nemuno*; it is a theme that resonates with certainty in much of his poetry; and it is motivation that has led him to the liberation movement and government service in two areas—education and culture—which he believes are essential to national amelioration as well as personal redemption.

Because of his broad cultural engagements and interests, or perhaps because his aesthetic and personal predilections have propelled him to such engagements beyond the realm of poetic intersections with the world, Platelis encourages all of us—as a human collective and as a gathering of responsible individuals—to accept an active role in forging an ethical sense of self within an enlightened moral and cultural context.

These elements reflect a distinctive postmodernist strain in his work. Like a handful of other postmodernists on the contemporary poetic stage in Lithuania, Platelis also hides behind masks of his own creation, not because he does not believe in the ethical values he professes but because he does not believe in the act of such profession or in the ultimate validity of the professor. Such proclamations, after all, are human in their dimension, and in his poems Platelis knows that his imaginings are conditional, that his ability to render a complicated and multilayered reality in absolute terms is imperfect. He alternates masks, presents and explores various voices, confirms a breadth of perspectives and angles of reflection in his work, all the while inviting us to immerse ourselves in the voices that call out to us, to follow along.

Platelis' poetry is important for other reasons as well, not the least of which are his sense of the overwhelming power of history and his understanding and exposition of its Orwellian dimensions. What saves us all, he says, in the dark light of such madness, is the possibility that we can indeed discover counterpoints to spiritual terror. Those counterpoints, which can shape individual lives and the nation's existence for the good, can be found in the affirmation of the role played by love and by the imagination in combating the legacy of fear and alienation that has defined the postwar Lithuanian experience and, in fact, which has foundationally shaped human civilization.

In Platelis' poetry, the powers of love and of imagination often work in concert and in the face of difficult odds to sustain the human heart and spirit. The result is transcendence and Platelis provides lucid touchstones on that journey. By encouraging, in his own persuasive way, opportunities for personal as well as social liberation and freedom, and the individual as well as collective ethical realignment such opportunities make possible, Platelis has rightfully earned a prominent place among the European writers of his generation.

I have included poems from all of Platelis' published collections in this book. Some of these translations date back more than thirty-five years and were made during the early stages of our friendship and literary collaboration. It is a joy to remember working with him then, just as it has been a continuing joy to work with him across the span of all these years.

As I gathered the translations I had made into these pages, I thought it important to add additional translations as well, many of them new poems from Platelis' latest books and some older poems from earlier books that now seem to me to be important and defining expressions of the constants as well as of the evolutions in his poetic career. I was guided in that process by suggestions and conversations with Platelis himself, through letters and emails and in person during my visits to his home and his visits to mine. I am most grateful for his cooperation and encouragement during the course of my work. So this book is my collected translation of his poems, the definitive presentation of his work in English. I could not have asked for a more gracious or engaged partner in the process of presenting that work in ways in which I believed his poems speak and sing most clearly.

J.Z.

I

the rain to the ground
the raven browsing the scrapheap
an April morning

The Carpet on the Wall

There is a clear stream, hurrying briskly from the hill to the valley,
Curling over rocks and dividing the sleepy landscape
Into two halves, separating the family of deer from
The small white house under drooping spruce branches.

Succulent grass and quiet hills snugly surround
The woodcutter's white homestead, but there's no sign of the man
Who has just awakened and probably looks through the window
At the quietly murmuring brook and the deer drinking there.

As I am, just waking and seeing the wall and the carpet,
That's why for a moment or two I may not return from dream's
Pleasant seclusion, from the silence that even the threads protect,
Faded from the years and from my drowsy glances.

But work will not wait—creaking it raises the sun,
The man will soon go out and the deer will vanish in the hills,
My tired joints will sink into the clamor of the day,
And the old simple carpet until morning will long for me.

May, 1977

Milk and Tomatoes

she left a note: dearest
buy two bottles of milk and two
tomatoes he thought for a long time
having read the note sitting on the kitchen
stool how white milk is in a glass
creamy and white
as the skin of her face
it will flow past lips into the belly
then she will wipe herself with a white
napkin while tomatoes
are red as lips their juice
flows down the marble chin
until a white hand wipes it away
(tomatoes are so juicy!)
her eyes will shine with desire
she will be wearing a white dress
or a checked skirt

he will definitely buy
two bottles of milk and two
tomatoes

August, 1978

The Runner

The mirror's cold glass opens.
She runs through the long gallery from column to column,
Covering her eyes against the clear spring sun,
An unfamiliar wind
Flutters her hair and lifts the bright red
Silk garment, lady,
That bloody spring blossoming of roses is for you
(In niches angry armor morally lowers its visors),
The wind is anxious, passionately
Kissing the golden skin
Of thighs, like peaches ripening in the sun.
It is a royal wind, she runs
Down the Renaissance gallery into the center of the palace
Where her numb lover waits
Among moths immune to naphthalene, decorative
Rugs, weapons on the wall
That forgot the warmth of hands.
She runs through the sweltering swoon of summer,
Her garment tears, her breasts break through trembling—
Their fragrance is as intoxicating as wine—and she runs
Through autumn, rustling in multicolored leaves,
The wind blows, tearing off the last
Bit of clothing, violent drops of rain
Cut her fertile belly.
She stands
Holding her breath in the cold winter moonlight,
Her bare lips blurt out something about death,
Her face is hoary with frost. Poetically. Lady,
This rosy blossoming of blood is yours,
Open the door—the king
Is waiting.

Secret shadows from the candle fall onto the screen,
Servant girls with graceful gestures fill the space
Above the dark pool's arena, melancholy lotuses

Bob on the fragrant water, I—
A boy in short pants with an old wrinkled face
(Flaming eyes—all the life in this body)—
Slink through the shadows of house plants and then—
The candle flame flickers, it rises above the pool
Divinely naked and wades into the water,
Fog lifts...

It is a poetic fog. Shadows catch the rhythm,
Everything sways and leaps, even the heaviest thoughts,
But the oval of the face touches the black surface of the water...
The candles burn out. In the dark.
What word will penetrate here, what lips will utter it,
In whose name do I dare, alone in the dark and nameless,
To disturb the silence full of whispering and shaking?
Here is the earth. Fog rises before morning.
It is a poetic fog.
Between the moths and naphthalene, between reality and sensation,
Nowhere or everywhere, in the veins of the runner.
The king waits.
Entrez.
She crosses the threshold
Smelling of water and pollen.
Picks up the zither. Sounds spill in the cold.
A cool hand like a crow settles on her shoulder
And slides downward until a cool instant of eternity
Embraces the mute waist. On the edge of the abyss.
Blued fingertips penetrate the white skin.
It is a royal cold. Entrez.
The king crosses the threshold.

February, 1979

An Encounter at Dusk

While looking out the library window
At the dusk of winter,
The shelves suddenly open and a boy enters
Carrying a basket of apples and roses.
And the darkness thickens, thoughts tangle.
Today—he says—
A very strange thing happened to me:
I was walking down the orchard path and found myself
In a gloomy room with shelves,
Filled with rectangular slabs.
A sad man stood there looking out the window
At the dusk of winter.

November, 1983

Seaside Quartet

I could easily open my heart to my beloved.
All spoken words are cloaked with untruth,
Remembered pasts, perceived realities.
I could easily whisper everything to my beloved at the ocean's edge,
Into the small shell of her ear
Which has just cast out a pearl...
But midday draws near and a man in long robes
Says to a small boy carrying the ocean in pails
To a small hole in the sand that it is senseless, but my beloved
Answers that waters flow in a circle and fill the living
While words...
While words also flow in a circle, my love,
Against the current.

November, 1982

Tiresias

I—only one half of knowledge with a heavy pelvis,
With passive wisdom, holding imprisoned
Within myself the only man.
I define the future with words.
(That which you ask for, Hera,
Is most difficult for me to separate, because the truest thoughts
Exist on their own: they make love, reproduce, and surely
Feel pleasure.) My ears are open
And the air is full of whispers and the roads
Full of travelers. I—a blind woman
Along the road. Beggars cast their seed into me.
This body is pregnant with the past, breasts heavy with the future.
Aphrodite herself distinguishes shapes, Zeus,
To bring them to union again.
You know where gender is obliterated
And you know where my real face is.
On the other side of sensation, on the other side of thought...
I do not know which.

July, 1980

A Poem About Solitary Architecture

Stiff towers in the long autumn rain
Pierce the stony sky.
Pigeons and crows find shelter there
From the city's noise.
Half-savage cats
Read the letters of rooftops and walls, swallows
Understand fully the conversations of ledges.
A cold wind walks the archways,
Fingers the pediments,
Measures the width of columns, ponders
The symbolism of plans and façades.
And throws into my eyes
The fine dust of disintegration—the only common language
That I know
And is known by the long loneliness of these buildings.

October, 1982

Overtaken Fog

Her golden hair
Flames like the first sacrifice of harvest in the green fields
And her feet glitter like sparkles.

Overtake her. (The moment of union intoxicating —
It is the inconceivable realization of form,
The lightning-quick "yes" and the thunder
Immediately echoing.)
Overtake her with words?

Her feet suddenly sink into the soft ground.
Her hands turn to branches.
Her gentle waist is covered by coarse bark (the present
Grows strangely between her ribs)—a laurel tree.

And the days grow brighter,
Joy penetrates the joints
Like evening fog on the river.

August, 1982

The Glance

She pushes through dark dust-filled rooms
In a white wedding gown to a space washed in sunlight,
Explodes like a clear ball of fire from
Along the line of dark buildings like the seasons, runs
Into a pleasant square framed by bindweed,
Glancing covetously for the last time
At a light-haired young man with St. George's spear
On a white restless steed
That will soon gallop through the thin curtain of death
Into an eternal morning,
Into a life that will immediately
Begin (everyone waits
Stretched to witness) and so—
Her eyes widens like two large caverns,
The dust-filled square already sinks down in menace,
Spurs press the steed and it heaves through the forehead,
Striking a spark of pain
And disappears on the other side of memory's intricate ornament.
Stains of blood spatter the soul's white linens.

October, 1981

Pastoral

She comes near the water, insidiously takes off her clothes
As if not feeling the congealed stare in the rushes.
Her legs are as strong as the posts of the city's gates,
Her skin sealed tight as my prison's wall,
A brickwork of the iron of hours and fear.
Beneath the silks of leaves, among soft rocks,
I watch the quieting sea—the holy sun
Doubles in motley eyes like the breasts of a goddess
And sinks slowly into the red water of evening.

But you barely manage to go out to dance in your bodies,
Bewitchingly radiant, my tongue goes numb
And feet take root in the fascinated stones.
It is music and light, the mysterious
Brook, filling all the most noble forms
And flowing toward the side of thirst
With streams of milk and honey, it is a cloud
Whose every curl promises you
The illusion of immortality
And an easy road downward with the seeds and petals.
Moist One, Powerful One, Most Pure!

June, 1982

ZDANYS

The Raven

Most often it caws in the middle of the night
When the world is sunk deeply into the swampy
Kingdom of darkness and no voice
Stumbles behind things. And it vibrates
The thick walls of being, but not in the way
That E.A. Poe heard but with the small trumpets
Of a miniature Jericho—the clothing tears
And when it's gone a quiet resident remains
Who, waking, finds the television on,
A carpet with a cigarette burnt hole, and had forgotten
To take off the wrinkled formal wear—
NEVERMORE.

September, 1979

My Grandmother's History

In the corner, aloe.
She had round-rimmed glasses.
A cat mewled beneath her window
And dust settled on her gramophone.
Talking about the past she would say: consummatum est
or something else in Latin.
She especially loved one philosopher. Caligula, I think.
But we were so involved in this world...

When she died
I inherited everything.
Most important, the gramophone on which I would play
Popular songs until I went mad,
And the cat beneath the window, in which in the evening
Sunsets glowed, and for the first time
I experienced how old the world is.
Even before proclaiming myself divine.
And later my gramophonic mouth matured,
My thoughts cleared, and my whole body
Mewled sadly whenever its surface
Was touched by the fingers of aloe-tinged memories,
And divine dreams danced in the dust of madness—
Such sweetness!

Perhaps the world is older than my grandmother—
I said scattered among its shapes—
If the soul melted without overcoming resistance
And gives itself victories only at night
In erotic twilights. And in the end
I understood how hard the road was
That led from my grandmother's house,
What angry god gave us our hopes and days.

And songs played on the gramophone also grew old,
Went out of style, and the cells of my body,

ZDANYS

Having turned to dust, so dulled the needle
That in the evenings I began to drink boiled milk

And trembling with pleasure
Watched my neighbors' lives.

The hours are so deep, and if
My grandmother had sunken into them without pain
She would have much to be grateful for
To the healing properties of aloe.

August, 1979

Restorers

We found a dancing foot in the tall grass.
A marble girl must have lost it, running
At night through our forests.
Sunset reddened her white glittering calf,
Of the kind only a goddess could have. Our breasts
Instantly filled with the power to recreate all of her,
So we quickly began
To form her missing joints from bee's wax,
Clinging to her like a litter of piglets.
We talked incantations, drew secret tokens,
Until the desired image
Began to shine in our foggy retinas.
She was like a goddess—long hair the color of wheat,
A young body coming clear under her thin garment,
Her hips trembled barely visibly,
Tense with a congealed hot wild dance.
Someone said the Our Father, someone wept.
We saw a flame
Pulsating beneath her thin skin, her breast
Rising with her breathing, the cunning soft stirring of her lips.
Because suddenly terror and madness flooded our veins,
Hands reaching for her paying no heed to our wills.
We held one another until consciousness did not abandon us.
Then we sang songs of love, angrily
Raising our fists to the emptied heavens.
(The world went on without us, we were not ourselves.)
And after that we began
To beat each other and when we saw first blood
We grabbed our axes.
Only one victor was left alive.
Under a clear midday sun
And the cold shine of the goddess' smile. All
Red with blood. He threw down his ax and shyly
Embraced the girl's slender waist.

Wax
Suddenly melted from the endless heat of his heart.
Yellow streams flowed down his face, shoulders, stretched
Down his torso until it covered all of him
And stiffened to bronze.

May, 1983

The Miracle of Wine

Then we walked inside through the fortress' low
Gates. The rocking yard
Was full of drunken soldiers, loud women,
Worried servants. The smell of death
And cooking food hung in the air. Infants cried.
We turned straight into the tavern. It was
A dark cellar with hides covering the walls.
My fiancée
Asked for supper, and a fat red-faced innkeeper
Came forward with a servant carrying a jug of wine
And a roasting spit dripping dark liquid.
And one drop splashed on my companion
And suddenly our table was covered with ripe fruits:
Grapes
Fell into my fiancée's lap. Thick juices
Flowed down her thighs, bread and meat appeared.
We raised our glasses for our life to come,
And while we drank, touching our foreheads and knees,
Splashing like fish in the lakes of each other's eyes,
Bunches of grapes sprouted long stems,
Shoots wound around our legs, heavy ears
Of rye sprouted from the bread, the pig
Jumped from the serving tray squealing "hyes."
Fear cut our tendons. The feasters
Covetously stared at us with unreadable glances
But we quickly began to eat and—it seems—
Nothing happened: the spring
Night unfolded, we drew near the rocks of an unknown shore.
All around flamed torches. Someone
Constantly asked me my name. A few soldiers
Cocked their eyes at me, talking about something.
And when, for the last time,
I renounced myself, they surrounded us
With a circle of burning stares, a wall
Of drool-covered chins, a cupola of trembling hands...

But my beloved tosses her yellow hair
And suddenly a ship grows into the sea, terror
Widens the pupils of our eyes, wine covers the deck,
Horrible divine wine like blood of a raging bull,
Like the voice of a lion in the brambles of an overgrown ship.
They leap into the water—
Perfect fish of the flood—they explode in the shoreless sea
In all seven directions, they
Fly in fiery shuttles to the other side of the horizon
And weave a new water, and land, and sky!
Foaming torrents wash the old forms,
Things do not find names behind the suddenly dropped veil,
Hearts filled with power at the great crossroads
Fuse reality into a pearl and close themselves up inside it...

The water around boiled with fish,
The air paled with birds.
Their firm joy tore the hearts of sailors
Like young wine old casks, having carried many harvests,
And the one that did not tear spoiled beneath stony
Arches of chests and turned to vinegar
And fell, closing the circle,
On lips that planted the vineyard seed. They
Jumped from the ship, singing softly to mermaids:
"He who turns water to wine will have his blood
Turned to water." And before touching
The primal mother's foaming lap
They became beings of the new world.

And the waves slowly quieted, diluting
Red streams, the current carried away the shoots.
My fiancée
Sat half-reclining, leaning against the mast,
With tousled hair, torn clothing,
With a wound under her right breast.
Blood dripped to the deck
Spattered with milt and hard-roe
Drying in the morning sun.

April, 1983

The Wedding Procession

While returning to town,
Near the gates, my bride suddenly stopped the procession
And asked me how a person
Is born and I answered: mistress,
Love is that third which unites two into one:
You stretch out across the dark unspoken valleys,
Heavy moonlight inundates rippled plains,
I draw near filled with the power of love,
Hair glittering in the sun shakes like a lion's mane,
And suddenly an obvious rhythm fills the stagnant body
And from the depths of darkness
Arises a terrible power, a whirlwind hissing like a serpent,
Hurls itself into the shapes of thought
And the gates crumble.
That's how a person is born and is born again...

The drums rattled and the flutes squeaked shrilly,
Long flags waved in the towers.
The eighth gate
Opened wide and the town swallowed us like my bride's
Bottomless smile. Grass scattered from her face.
In the coach's black corner I began to kiss her—o my
White lambkin!—but the wheel
Suddenly caught on the gate's cornerstone—
I was lifted upwards, she cast down.

Now across black water
I return to the wedding procession (everything
Which is worth singing of—is the joy of uniting),
Return through the labyrinths of nonexistence to my bride's refuge.
Ah, from two is born one—she sings quietly in the mist
In a witch's voice her heavy and tenacious wisdom,
Like collapsing earth, like gates closing in the darkness.

March, 1983

The Way of Flax

Sister, our days are ending, only air and earth remain,
Life returns to seed, time returns to the beginning,
Our journey is ending—across fields torn by wind
The Archer carries a bow to shoot the years' arrow into the sky.

A seed of flax I fell into the powerful beginning of spring,
A young ram, white-wooled from father Vaižgantas' hand,
Azure skies enveloped me, the Sun and Moon quickly
Locked me up with the key of time, covered me carefully with soil.
I sprouted from small truthful clothes, easily attracted
By wet and warm Žemyna's, our primal mother's, body,
Tearing asunder comfortable armor, I rose to a foreign sky;
Its storms tossed my stem, its waters washed my face.
I took a woman to wife when the time came, blooming
Blue I stood mute in the wind of dawn,
Had a throng of children, as the fertile Moon fated,
As the generous Sun warmed me and Žemyna fed me.

When Libra rose, you tore me away from my world,
From my round poor existence, embraced by roots,
And set me swaddled, feet up to the cooling firmament,
So my heart would awaken from sleep, so my thoughts would learn
To feed on sap and take root like the eternal grass.
You brushed away my family, broke the threads
That held me to my relations, opened true things to the light of my eyes.
I was retting in the moonlit pond until my soul,
Separated from my joints, readied itself to fly off with the birds.
I lay senseless in the wind which carried my sap,
Touched by fire, to the Sun, to the waters of heaven.

Sister, my suffering is ending, you have only to break
The delicate shell, which carried the frail life it enclosed,
And brush the linen's boons to the sodden soil.
Begin the great task, as the signs of eternal constellations command:

Comb the fiber neatly and spin it into the thinnest threads,
Then weave us straight into the heavens, into the greatest
Bones of worlds, into the works of the living repeating love and truth.

November, 1982

* *Vaižgantas—the god of flax in Lithuanian mythology.*
Žemyna—Lithuanian goddess of earth, soil, vegetation, and fertility.
The Sun is female and the Moon is male in the Lithuanian language and mythology.

Proteus

Consciousness loses its way among the words of lies
In day's delusions and night's metaphors.
At the crossroads
I set a trap for the beast.
At night the weather vane creaked,
Someone weeping in an owl's voice
Tossed about in the spiderwebs of my contemplations.

What can I say to the man who strangles me?
What face do I reveal? Masks like wet snow
Fall and melt on his dirty hands,
On the paws of everyday,
That reek of bodies, food,
The sweat of nerves.

Tracks of a strange beast,
Ropes burst apart,
Morning dew on paper—
My face?

October, 1983

Midday

A light wind ripples through the wild poppy
Blossoms, brushes across my face
With the fragrance of drying straw, reminding me
Of love's promises in the shade of blooming lindens.
The clouds are like tangled bodies
On pale blue sheets.
I asked suddenly:
Midday, where is your essence?
And it answered me: in this grass among blossoming
Wild poppies, in the skull of a sitting man,
In that skull are many gray cells, in those
Cells many words, among those words—one
Which is my essence, but no one
Knows it: not that man nor I.

September, 1985

The Forests' Betrothed

My lips crack and thoughts crumble
From the heat.
A dry wind, breaking free
From a flaming sky,
Casts a cloud of pollen into my face.
Fine yellowish powder
Covers my black suit, shoes and hat.
I switch my suitcase to my left hand
And beat myself like a penitent with a bird-cherry branch
Until I approach the cottage.
Who are you?—the doorway sphinx asks,
And I answer: the forests'
Betrothed.

July, 1983

Breaking Glass

When I see you walking by
Easy and short-lived
As a morning in May
And I want to call you, touch you, stop you,
Those who live with me,
Standing just over my shoulder, sigh heavily
With cold breath on my back.

And my head droops,
My voice freezes in my mouth,
The smile fades from my lips.

Only my hand, as if on its own, stutters toward you
Brushing against the flasks,
And the sound of breaking glass fills the room.

You disappear beyond the misty edge of consciousness
Frightened by the noise,
Muse of the poetry of love.

May, 1985

Secret Conversations

You talk and talk, having forgotten
That you are talking with the dead.
Their words shape their faces,
Their thoughts quicken your blood,
And someone begins to talk to you
As if talking to the dead.

Horizons of the living murmur
With the monotone drone of the sea.

July, 1984

The Descending Swan

Into the pond's mirror
A swan descends silently
And its reflection
Perches on the bottom of evening
And its black feet
Touch the top of the water
And both swans melt into one.

Bending down you whisper something to me without a sound
Then put your head on my shoulder
And disappear behind the fluttering shroud of dreams.

April, 1984

Melancholy

She cannot rebel or protest,
Enveloped in endless dejection,
Looking through the window
At the March snow, silent,
Requiring nothing from me,
As if she had died,
My soul.

November, 1984

Confession

I long for the days when my powerful arm grabbed
A woman by the waist and sat her on a fireblood steed
And the earth thundered beneath its light hoofs,
And the sword stood guard at my side
Ready at each blink of the eye
To defend me against persecutors,
To win food for her, soft silks,
Ornaments of gold.
And no one inside me would dare object
When I shouted: I Desire!

April, 1985

A Quiet Evening

Holding one another's hands
Looking into one another's eyes
We stand in the soft evening light
After a long kiss.

Suddenly a large moth
With drooping wings of lace
Descends between us,
Dusting our faces with the sticky powder of its wings.
"Ah love," you say, "ah destiny!"
The whole world smells.

July, 1984

The Cut

The cut that opens midday
Reveals the clean
Cloth of our shared existence
In which life's juices pulsate,
Souls' secret conspiracies shine.
While the day's entire bustling,
In the name of shelter and food,
Power and physical love,
Is a reflection of death's kingdom
In the mirror of life.

June, 1984

Starlings

My son asked me to build a bird house
For a starling and we worked together hard
All afternoon to build it properly
And cut and planed and shaped the boards.
And so the house outside the window here.
The starling is expecting children, whistles
Every morning on the birdhouse pole, while
I sit at my desk and write down something
Believing that the two of us are kin
And that our dedicated trills and songs
Spread out through different communities
Though the meaning is probably the same.

April, 1984

Czech Etude

Tobacco smoke
Billows among the tables like a river
Across the stones of heads. On a small round table
A glass of beer and cooked liver sausage.
A pale woman quietly approaches
And tugs on my sleeve.
My eyes are locked on the haunches of a waitress,
My mouth full of fatty cud, my fingers convulsively
Fondle the glass' handle, but she approaches
Once again and says: it's time
And we go out into the wet autumnal street.

Each journey is like a death
And poetry—says the young man dressed in black
In the violet rain by the door—
You leave the cozy tavern,
Your comfortable circle of drinking friends, only to
Wake up in a cold room among scattered masks,
Torn formal wear,
Things ravaged by the whirlwind of passion,
Alongside the woman who sleeps enigmatically,
The white oval of her face turned to the moon.
Before dawn the man gets up, lights a cigarette,
Walks across the cell, persistently looking for the door.
As the sun rises this room
Begins to look like an office
Which could best be described by the gloomy and pedantic
Jew from Prague, Joseph K.,
And in the evening, once again a tavern
Where thick-hipped
Romantic poetesses force you to feel
Love for the world of things.
But the woman is only one—
Says the young man, wiping his lips
With a fragrant handkerchief.

ZDANYS

The one who wakes in late afternoon, stretches, gets up,
Goes out of the rib cage with predacious steps.
One like a journey
From birth to death.

February, 1984

Periplum

Longing for a world
Not abandoned by gods makes us dizzy
As we dissect the dream's foaming waters.
Ancient supple bodies of waves writhe beneath the keel.
The XXth century
Opens off starboard:
Great numbers of vistas that capture the eyes,
Friendly and hostile ports, dangerous cliffs,
Islands filled with tourists.
On this side gods and goddesses protect each
Of our movements, but there
The struggle for daily bread, buying and selling,
Clever usurers and politicians deep in debt,
Powerful perfidious empires,
Forbidden zones, hiding not the painful
Questions of belief and morality
But military bases with nuclear missiles,
Containers of chemical and biological weapons,
Lasers and psychotropic drugs.
We have been returning from Troy all these years,
Conquerors and the conquered,
Oppressed by a common curse. We return
And at home discover the wiles that await us
And in nearly every port
They tell us of a new City's capitulation.

And so — the ship's crew rests on a small island
Whose name we do not even know.
Ulysseans sometimes stray over to it,
Convert the signs of death's kingdom to water and food
And try to convince us that the sound mind of the Enlightenment
Has forgotten its ethical principles
And has become a weapon in the sophists' hands.
But they never get on boats and never travel,
They have filled their firm continents

With fantastic lunaparks
Not suitable for living or dying.
Our ancestor was wise and so did not waste time
Deliberating if events were unfolding properly, did not impose
His measure of reality.
He searched for balance between sea
And land in his own destiny. While the residents on shore
Are busy inheriting nations and countries
From the generation that fought the Second World War
And threaten one another again with shining weapons.

Densely populated places, beaches and harbors
Float past starboard...
But each can find for himself the balance
Between land and sea and there
Build his own beliefs.
Like our ancestor, who successfully traversed the seas,
Not avoiding curses, only retribution,
Captain Nothing.
Though we are already condemned to the sea and generously built
Cenotaphs of words on rocky promontories.
That is why, floating on this peculiar vessel,
We can feel this absurd longing for a pure world,
A gentle girlish longing,
And can hope to exchange it in some harbor
For water and food
Having paid the customs duty to usurers.

December, 1985

Ghosts

> *Therefore when Tao is lost, there is Te.*
> *When Te is lost, there is kindness.*
> *When kindness is lost, there is justice.*
> *When justice is lost, there is ritual.*
> *Now ritual is the husk of faith and loyalty,*
> *the beginning of confusion.*
> Lao Tse. *Tao Te Ching, 38*

Paris.
The train comes to a slow stop, blows steam,
The conductor gives the signal, rational
Lawyers shout "hoorah"—Kung Tse climbs down the stairs
Smiling mysteriously. Then the orchestra
Bangs in such a way that the visitor squats frightened
And scatters his principles of harmony.
It's the end of the 18th century—sentimental
Burghers, clean rivers, fields fertilized with manure...

But then the emperor
Ch'in Shih Huang Ti decides for all time
From the heights of Mo Tse's teachings
To criticize Confucius' supporters, that's why they
Are buried alive in the ground and quickly suffocate
Under the happy Empire's body—
The correction of names, the correction of lives
According to the matrices of death... Although words
Swell quickly with blood and become as sluggish
As satiated ticks.

And only the accomplices of the buried
Swiftly cut the ropes and head for the mountains,
On every road watched by the emperor's horsemen.
Donkeys carry rolls of books.
And later from Tibet we receive a note
In which the escapees, having rummaged through their brains,

Demand orators
Who explain the ritual only from aesthetic and ethical perspectives,
Punish with physical punishments—
Twenty strokes of bamboo sticks on each sole.

The dragon is reborn from its own
Ashes. At first so beautiful and kind,
So pure and attractive,
Swinging in the bodies of sages, having secured itself
Between the word and consciousness.
And works its way through all barriers
Like the virus of typhoid fever.
And then it is too late—bile floods
Our desolate hearts and famished teachings
Incarnate themselves in real time: at night
Black echelons begin to move from darkened stations
To nowhere, unloading the dead
Along the way like mail. And our
(Association of Ghosts) chancellery
Doesn't manage to stamp the personal
Papers of all the spirits...

And all that is missing is one basketful
To complete the mountain
And the world rolls forward
Along its only road
And the dead are not connected to these things,
Completely not connected.

October, 1984

An Empty House

The floor creaks sharply
As I walk through the house,
The door groans, the cuckoo,
Popping out of the rusted clock,
Sings three times into the deaf afternoon
And a pale boy
Casts an angry glance at me
From around the corner.

That's how we meet in our indivisible land—
A man from the marketplace and a lost giant—
Beneath a sun setting into dust.
A rock like a bolt of lightning
Cuts the thick air, and slain I fall
Face down into my ancestors' cold ashes.

An empty house. On the window sill
A vase with the hyacinth
Of my pagan soul. The spring wind
Suddenly blows in through the broken window
And stirs the ashes in the hearth.

September, 1983

Morning Concert

The sun cascades into the littered room
Through dirty curtains.
A table splashed with beer where several naiads
Sleep with their heads resting
Among scraps of food. A young man
Blows on a jabbering flute. She brings over
A tub of water, puts it on the dirty floor and slowly
Begins to undress. The music teacher
Starts to play a monotonous song. She puts
Her left foot into the water, bends over and...
My body suddenly shivers, my face reddens,
Hot steam through the nostrils bristles the hair of those still sleeping,
The hardening forehead aches, fists turn into hooves,
A holy picture falls from the wall caught by a horn
And breaks into a thousand mirror splinters.
What did I see, God, what did I see?
It's a miraculous sign involuntarily and unintentionally
Opening the secrets of the world and heart,
The sources of truth and power!
Things brighten, there is a fragrance of incense.
The head is wrapped in the stiff ringing of space.

Dogs barked terrifyingly outside.
The teacher choked on a sound,
The young man threw away the flute.
I tried to speak but the two of them
Gaped at each other and squealed like pigs.
Deer—I thought—only deer in forest valleys
Could understand the meaning of lofty words.
Then—through the door out
Into the bright autumnal air. Hounds
Cling to the joints. No one
Will know I am forced to leave my body
To the red jaws of dogs.
Together with the instruments of speech.

Together with the will to speak.
Blood spatters the grass.
A net of curtains.
A gate of forged iron.
Time slamming shut.

June, 1984

ZDANYS

Forest Duel

Legs sink to the knees in the soft snow.
Trees beneath a weight of white.
A frozen winter morning.
Suddenly, he leaps from under the bush
Into the middle of the glade. In a flash
Swords leave their sheaths,
Cloaks fall down around the feet.
A pure ringing of metal
And our short cries quiver the air.
Snows falls from the trees.

Later—a moment of oblivion,
A delayed, lost moment,
And the shining blades slide across my neck.
Blood paints the snow.
Sleep through the artery of sleep floods the brain.
He leaves with my shield,
My symbol,
And carries my face toward the land of the living.

August, 1984

While Sifting Through the Pile of Slag I Find a Beer Bottle Cap

My distant brother, I see how you turn over the first container and wipe
    The cold perspiration off
        Looking ahead with a scowl.
Your mouth is getting dry, your head is pounding, your heart gallops strangely because
    Of the bottle of vodka that
        Last night flooded you.
You pull a bottle of beer carefully out from the deep pocket of your work wear.
    All around you loom the tall
        Mountains of stinking slag.
You press the bottle cap with the palm of your hand, holding it firm against an oily board
    And from the bottle neck white
        Foam bubbles out in a smile.
Head tipped back and not hesitating you drink down half of the liquid
    And concentrating listen
        To the changes in your gut—
To be or not to be, you deliberate and then rising back to the surface
    You finish the remaining
        Beer and burp happily.
The bottle cap remains in the slag, and loaded into the truck
    It flies with the wind, where I
        Hold a heavy shovel up.
Rapidly motioning with it back and forth I uncover your silent letter—
    The friendly smile of the sun
        Glitters in this heap of slag.

December, 1983

An Epic Poet in Spring

A cold November fog covers the windows.
Even at midday
You can barely make out the letters.
In the corner rusting armor, chipped blades of the sword.
The hero is laid out in the hall. An old woman
Occasionally replaces the candles. With arms lowered
I walk out into the sunlit garden, into spring.
Handsome young men and blossoming women
Whisper to one another in small groups.
My voice is hoarse from songs of the march
And my eyes are filled with revulsion.
What to say and to whom?
Everyone whispers about their own concerns.
The most important— nasty games of love.
Nature is engaged in its own renewal.
Words are full of indecent remarks.
"That is to say, everything is possible?"
I ask, holding before my eyes a perforated helmet
As if the skull of Yorick.

April, 1985

War's Beginning

The beginning of every great war is beautiful: orchestras,
Snappy uniforms, the pounding of steps on the roadway
Like the pulsing of the heart
Coursing the nation's strong blood
Through the indivisible network of veins,
Shining weapons
And eyes, and lightness beneath the heart
Which is felt by a piercing falcon
Or an arrow flying toward the target, or a fist
Between intention and blow...
The beginning of every great war is beautiful.
Who at such a moment would think about war?

July, 1984

Sunrise

God's face illuminates our
Quieting souls. Flames and flags cast
Reflections on the soldiers' faces. The weapons' blades
Gleam, polished during long hours of night.
Restive horses trample in place. The nomads'
Wedge is directed at the dark lap of the forest.
But there is no death— we think leaning
On our shields that life
Roils in three worlds.
A hard road past savage lines
Of men, horses' bellies, the clanging of weapons,
The vulnerable body, past
The talk of prophets, sacred symbols, the form...
We are like dust in white
Clothing beneath the face of the rising sun
In the infinity of days— road dust.
And the Lord's foot is already lifted
And up ahead the panting of passing time
Soughs in the sacred groves.
And while
It has not set among us, while blood
Does not gush onto bleached linen shirts,
While the heavy odor of souls,
The cry of victory and the moans of the dying
Have not yet darkened the sun,
Let's watch
How it rises.

November, 1984

A Yotvingian's Prayer Riding to Fight the Enemy

Lord,
Here I am, still alive, but on my way
Out of your beautiful world, on the hard road to heaven,
Riding in front of your divine spear,
Repeating the dread song of victory and death.
My father blessed me
And my mother wept over me,
My sisters led my horse to the gates, my brothers
Rode with me to the forest.
I give my breath to your mercy
And pray you keep it in my breast as long as possible
So my spear could pierce bodies to my heart's content
And the steel of my sword could be sated.
Enemies billow like the sea, flooding our funerals.
We know: none of us will see how the Sun's
Rosy face touches the tops of the oak trees.
A thousand men
Like a fiery lance will pierce the enemy's army,
Straining muscles,
And will ride to the mountain, straight into heaven,
Followed by the souls of Crusaders, into the light,
Into the transparent light where our forefathers await us,
Where you, powerful Perkūnas,
Will look joyfully at the crowds of captives
And will laugh in a loud voice at their insidious god...
Although I do not know what place you will grant me
At your long table, or if I will
Be worthy to feast with your brave men,
I know you love your warriors, happily
Laying their heads beneath your feet,
And with a serene face you will accept our hot and intoxicating
Offering of blood, our white-faced souls,
Sacrificed to you by this earth, giving birth
To people and living things, in the place
Made holy by our lives and deeds...

ZDANYS

Lord,
We have finished our work in the valley of the living.
We have broken the strings of life, cut the bonds of pity.
Turn us into your lightning, into the spirit of vengeance,
The whirlwind of sacred fury,
And may each of our sighs be a black gust of death!

September, 1983

* *Yotvingians—an ancient Lithuanian tribe famous for its warriors. Perkūnas—the God of thunder, war, and energy in Lithuanian mythology.*

An Encounter in the Forest

The beaters and the dogs, as if in a painting,
Drink the first rays of the rising sun,
Morning, like a boar pierced by a shining spear,
Pours itself out in blood on the soft carpet of grass,
Horses snort in the grand frame of the landscape,
Birds sing. Suddenly
The voices of brass horns carve the sky,
Dew falls from the blossoms.
We march into the forest, blades of weapons flashing,
Dizzy with the prospect of the hunt.
The invigorating forest air shrouds us
Like an animal's final deep breath
Escaping from its foaming snout
And disappearing in our nostrils.

As we go deeper, a woman's shadow
Appears more frequently among the trees, enticing
Me to leave the hunting group... Somewhere in the distance
The horns and hounds and sounds of the beaters die out,
Fear begins to grip my heart.
Hundreds of threatening glances pierce the thicket of leaves,
Frightful rustling,
A raven's voice prophesying evil...
Flashes of divine beauty through consciousness
Desiring to immortalize them dim the mind...
The air is thick with spirits...

Suddenly she pops up in front of me,
Wearing a tunic of hides,
Žvoruna the bloody-handed, governess of the successful hunt,
Catches me by surprise, as if a child abandoned
By his mother having lost his way in the villages and fields.
My joints are fettered by terror and desire,
My hair stands on end, my eyes pop out of their sockets.
Carefully she grasps my neck with rough hands,

ZDANYS

Her nostrils flaring, eyes flaming, breast rapidly heaving.
She growls something softly, the way predatory doves coo.
Her body is as supple as a cat's
And her womb is imperious and greedy.
She takes my seed, not thinking about the living—
They are nothing,
At this moment their lives are lived out to the end,
There is only the future tense—the egg, pierced by lightning,
There is only the future,
The next step of the sun.

October, 1984

* Žvoruna—the goddess of wild beasts and hunting in Lithuanian mythology

Triptych with a Laughing Woman

I

A glance through the thicket of leaves scalds consciousness.
The sun in a drop of dew, the fragrance of grass,
The raven's piercing voice
Grows in significance
    becomes speech
For the fisher's frail body (beneath a cloak of ermine).
The lost carp
    leaps in the bright landscape
And drops again, leaving behind a golden glittering.

A glance through the thicket of leaves
    paralyzes the joints—
She separates herself from the trunks of trees.
From the brown-headed reeds
    that reach to her breasts.
The gold in her skin is like the gentleness
Of fruit, the air is heated with passion,
Drops of dew
    in the brown hair on her belly
Refract the shameless rays of light.

Drawing close she puts her hand
    on my chest and looks
Into my eyes the way the black eye
Of this pond stares into the depths of heaven.
And suddenly the landscape begins to tilt: the water pours
Over the banks, stipples your body... The quiet
Fluttering of fish, a flash of gold.
It is only
    water for washing—I assure myself—
    only water
Taking me into the luminous midday of existence,
Only living water

    (but why does a stream
Of blood writhe in it like a reddish snake?)
Only baptismal water, protecting
Against death, which hides behind every shape...
Only water,
    into which you take another step and
You flutter in the snares of the body,
Golden carp,
    fragrant wind of paradise!..

II

Sleep pours across consciousness in a sweet stream,
The sirens' song of oblivion fills my dreams,
Fish wander dizzy through coral caverns.
Your body's bottomless depths
Awaken desire, cruelty, fear, and again lull them to sleep.
In your breathing
    full of voices like a forest on a spring morning,
In the clouded pond of your eyes
    I can't recognize the reality I've known
        for so many years...

I say something in my dream, prove something
To someone with no ears,
Later a procession of pilgrims draws near in fours
With coarse Flemish faces,
    the decorations change.
My speech begins to crack
In air filled with sensuous sighs:
    to break away!
My arms and legs
Press against the softness of a woman's back,
Stiff masculine body,
The sharp maenadic nails leave red streaks
On my belly and chest,
The tart smell of sweat fills my nostrils...

Later... Two half-circles of her loins
Pressed in the soft grass, a snake
Lazily slithers from one to the other, thrusting out
Its two-pronged tongue...
Do you know that desire
When every cell
    feels itself separated
From the one loved,
Severed by a sharp sword
 and only through the power of fear
Holds within itself the fluid of life?
Do you know the body—
A single bed for a double soul? Night
Changes to day, while this ever-deeper sadness
    transfigures the instants of joy.

III

I often watch her in the morning, until she awakens,
Brushes a strand of golden hair from her face
And looks at me with frightened distrust
And then with a mocking smile...
Later we eat breakfast,
Pouring the milk of daily conversation for each other.
And I say in sudden anger:
    Salmacis!
(Drops of coffee splatter from our cups.)
Your bewitching likeness to the daughters of dreams
Enchants me and binds me with the fetters of love
Which are woven by my two-gendered soul
From the delicate webs of oblivion!
You hide death behind your glittering smile.
With shudder
    (and now too with passion) I remember
The other mandorla-like pond,
The treacherous snares
    the gods set for us
(And now—the fear of death),

ZDANYS

So we would be incarnated.
    Salmacis,
Who will show me the way out of you?
Doubled desires.
    Doubled speech.
She laughs loudly, head tilted back, splashing
The milky coffee on her breast. And my
Eyes watch her
    through a veil of desire
        and my
Spirit falls asleep murmuring: they
    are only words, only words, only words.

April, 1986

Country Morning

Fog above the field flogs against the shore of the yard,
Like a boat lost in the fog a cow bellows,
A pail rings out somewhere like a buoy bell,
The sun attempts to tear the curtains of mist,
A dog's chain rattles quietly
As it drags across the ground, pigs
Bristle in pens, geese cackle in the yard, a rooster crows,
Sheep bleat in the garden: armies
Of voices surround the quiet peaceful house,
Waves of sound beat against the windows,
Against the old woman's eardrums.
She prays silently
And perhaps listens to the divine song
Whispered to her by her God, because after a moment
She rises resolutely and marches off to the battlefield
With two pails...

And in this struggle wins
Her existence.

December, 1987

Christmas in the Forest

As evening fell we gathered in the juniper grove,
In the deep valley. And I was given
The gift of speech this night,
Comprehension. We selected
A full-branched tree in a small glade.
We sniffed its smells, on its branches
Hung small apples, carrots,
Dried mushrooms. Then raised
Our snouts to the moon and howled for half an hour
Until moonlight silvered the snow
On the branches and the stars
Delivered their masks: the Evening Star—
At the very top, others—for the branches
In place of candles... But how
To decorate the tree whose trunk
Turns into a backbone, on whose top a flower glows,
And at whose feet sleeps a serpent
Coiled into a triple ring? How can
It be made more beautiful? We polished our
Bloody fangs on the snow, the trees' bark,
And with the stinking warmth of our bodies
Melted the snow around it,
So out of the earth
Could crawl worms and moles,
Spiders and snakes, toads and frogs, so fish
Could swim out from underground rivers, in the end
The Serpent would slither in, would wind round
The prickly trunk proclaiming
The holidays' beginning—the birth
Of the new sun.

Later we ran in a circle around the tree
Howling, giddy
With joy and hunger.
We ate the snow, the bark of shrubs,
Last year's leaves, and afterwards swallowed
The tree's decorations
And attacked one another...

December, 1985

Intruders

Into the bright landscape
With blossoming plum trees drives a smoking
Jabbering bus, opens the door and shakes
Impatiently to swallow as fast as possible
Those few people in the station.
However, a girl of incoherent movements
(Not normal, in our opinion not having accepted
The uniform of consciousness we call reality)
Spreads her arms, jibs, moves off backwards.
Why is she being pushed here? Who is this greedy monster
That forced its way into this space filled with blossoms?
Why are they forcing her to climb into its stinking jaws,
Opening up like an accordion's bellows?
While the bus
Trembles ever more nervously together with its driver
As if both were linked together with a cardan shaft,
Had a single heart and brain.
They are sated. They're not interested in devouring
A few more people.
They lack patience, that's why the doors close
And the monster howling leaps forward
Leaving behind the girl who breathes
More easily, once more having avoided our reality,
Her mother, running after it with despair on her face
And waving the green branch of an unidentified tree,
Two or three people who wanted to let them pass,
The timid mumble of those perching in its belly,
The bright landscape with blossoming plums.

June, 1986

The Miracle of Blood

The village cemetery shudders as the rain begins
Wafting the fragrance of birch trees and lindens.
I hide beneath a wood-chip roof, back pressed
Against the chapel's cool boards
Turning gray from rain and sun.
Spirits gather here at night to pray.
Their priest turns invisible wine in a moldy chalice
To blood, like water after a long rain,
And gives it to his flock to drink.
It is a thick, soothing drink,
Constraining movement, pulling them
Back to their beds
To leave this world to the living
Who gather together each morning
With spades, pails, shoots of flowers
To arrange canopies...

That time, only rain rustled in the trees.
The dead slept soundly. Five girls walked
From the village, still very young,
Each carrying a bottle of cheap fortified wine
And sitting down in the chapel
Passed a glass around circling
Like the sun. The long rain bristled
Around them and the wine slowly
Turned to blood: their voices grew stronger,
They poured out words that were not in the language,
Gossiped about the affairs of their neighbors,
Complained that there was not even one
Suitable lad in the village
Because vodka had soured the seed
In their balls and it would be dangerous
To allow such guys to make children...
They talked like middle-aged women who had seen
Only the grayest half of reality.

ZDANYS

Some god in the dung-ruined wall
Where once an altar had stood listened
And blessed their innocent souls
And accepted their sacrifice and gave
Them communion
Through the apple wine, which then cost
One ruble seventeen.
And when they went away, leaving
Their bottles scattered on the floor,
The spirits quickly gathered to their evening prayers,
In holy and elevated moods,
Greeting me, patting me
On the back like old friends,
As they have never done before.

August, 1986

Zone

Where does it end, where does it begin?
Ventilation pipes on the flat roof drone
Like eternity. The landing force,
As they are called, climbs
On a metal truss that holds silos of sawdust,
To the chimney extending
From the varnishing shop, reach the top
And smell the terrifying mix of odors
That the ventilator vomits into the darkened sky,
Holding on to the metal beam
With arms and legs.
They hang that way until they shake off
This world and fall in
To the zone.

The physician's assistant, cursing,
Puts casts on arms and legs,
Wipes blistered lips
And noses with stinking ointment.
The landing force, as they are called,
One by one return in
To the zone.

January, 1987

Civil Defense Instructions

Along the path, by threes
Walk ladies dressed in blue coveralls,
The squad of fire fighters
Smokes, blowing thick smoke.
The Major, the leader of the Escadrille,
Lives a quiet epistolary life.
He is mentally unsound.
Everyone forgives him, even the sparrows
Chirp, hopping on the window ledge:
"We feel no hatred for you,
Major."

White sheets in the Hiroshima shrine,
Wreaths of flowers wilt, bells ring.
The Major writes letters to the world:
"Never, never again!"
(He is mentally unsound.)

The chain of assistance is ready:
Stretchers, bandages, gas masks.
Chatty tourists in Hiroshima
With temporarily spoiled attitudes
Stare at the Siamese twins and other monstrosities.
In the cities of the world demonstrators
Against war shout NO.
Ladies with gas masks
Run from right to left.
We feel no hatred
For Major Neveragain—he is not well.
The siren wails.

Kre kre—a raven
Flies across the sky.
Soon he will turn to nothing.

March, 1983

On the Other Side of the Glass

During the night frost
rewrote the landscape
in its own hand.

On fresh snow
only a black cat
with a white chest.

The forest has sunk into itself
while under thick ice
the river trickles silently.

"I"—like a mountain
in the river of perception
across the ice floes.

It snows on the waiting
orchard brides
in beggarly bits.

In the bowl of the silver
pond the moon
is like a round fish
between two lovers
who swallow it with their eyes

After a night rain
the garden fainted with joy,
dew in the calendula blossoms
shines with cathartic tears.

In the green ship
a deranged crew—the white
worm incites mutiny.

Across the night sky
a shrieking bird flew
from yesterday to tomorrow, from
the unknowable to the unknown.

And what sort of autumn is it without geese
making their way southwestward?
Yes, and here they are—
honk honk—barking away,
and we mark it down.

Leaves fall...
But first in the heart
the world passes away.

Pines with thin fingers
Comb the fog.
Muffled church bells
Fill their traces.

Wet tiles. Autumn.
Convolvulus
curls back into the ground.

A sad November morning—
the iron gates of my eyes
open as I wake.

December, 1987

For the Departing

You will not lose your way in the forest of life—
The mother of beasts
Will lead you through the warm brambles
Along gentle moaning valleys.

Do not fear if the air grows thick,
The bitter fragrance of the forest
Fills your lungs and the earth
Pulses and rocks beneath your feet.

You will not lose your way in the forest of night—
A woman dressed in black
But with a light heart will meet
You at the border of life.

And will take you down the beasts' path
Through hot, abundant springs,
Through warehouses of empty souls
To the new and welcoming shore.

October, 1987

Raise High the Mast, Carpenters!

Cracked boat shell—
Isn't it the one Gilgamesh used
To travel to that other shore,

To the land without time,
To the eternity of signs
Of a stiffened bolt of lightning?

Boards rot in the sand,
Speech and the soul die
In the valley of indecision.

The tree of language
Awaits the sap of our life,
The sails await our breathing.

Raise the mast, carpenters!
They return there as kings
With fruits made of diamonds.

June, 1987

The Girl and the Unicorn

Clear eyed, muzzle of the most precious velvet,
He lays his head on her lap. Graceful fingers
Sink slowly into the silken mane.

In the pleasant bower of the world
Among roses and cypress trees
Under a canopy of lilies.

Pain stitches her side,
The angel's thunderous voice
Overwhelms the drowsy heart—

A suspension bridge to the highest heights.

April, 1988

A Christmas Hymn

Quietly quietly
The sun rolls down
And hangs
On the bottom branches of the World's Spruce
Touched by the waves of the ocean of night.
Rejoice darkness!
Spew forth from your jaws armies of philosophers
And divisions of theosophists!
May they weave their nets of thought
With icy fingers
The way spiders knit the dark corners
Or rise against each other armed with tridents!
May they speak to the blind
About light, trying to present it
Through formulas, may they practice magic!
While it is still their time.
Because the Sun, having rocked
In the waves of nonexistence,
Begins to rise,
And God's light shines
On all worlds!
And spiders chase after retreating darkness,
Winding in their beliefs
Torn by flashes of light,
From the indescribable radiance
Which spreads from an unearthly man's golden face,
Flaming in a lion's mane,
Who is Surya and Savitri,
Mithra, Ra, Apollo, and Jesus Christ; the radiance
That spreads from an unearthly woman's face
In a wreath of flaxen hair,
Who is the Sun Mother
Raising everything that lives.

Let us all rejoice:
Here is the family by the cradle—
An earthly father and mother,
And beasts, speaking words.
The Child was born—
The bright hope of the world,
And the power of darkness
Will not conquer His soul.

Let us all rejoice:
Here is the family at the table
Breaking bread, sharing
Life and love.
The light of their spirits is absorbed by
The ornament on the tree
And the Sun in the depths of darkness
Gathers its strength to rise.

Let us all rejoice,
Here for the birth of God,
Those whose hearts are free
Of anger and hatred,
Whose father is God
And whose mother is Earth,
Whose brother—the world
And sister—life!

Let us rejoice, whose blood pulses
According to mathematical formulas and rational truths,
Whose minds see reality so clearly
And who explain it so academically
That they do not see themselves.
We are fortunate to have feelings
Which absorb the Sun's light
And pass it on to souls
Without disturbing the order of mind.

Let us rejoice for whom this world is a commodity,
For whom gold is god and profits more precious than truth:
Usurers counting money
Will burn less electricity.
It will be easier for
Informers and executioners
To do their work with the people!

Let us rejoice who hate
Themselves and others and God—
Unfortunate minds do not stop
The approaching Sun's light!
And this winter will pass,
The world will turn green
And the Child will be born for us
With eyes opened wide!

Let us all rejoice, the moral and the sinners,
Those who hold themselves moral
And those who call themselves sinners!
Let us welcome one another
Into each of our hearts
The way the Sun rises for all
Without rejecting any!

At least for a moment
Today
Let us feel the great oneness
Which even without our knowing
Is.

December, 1987

The Start of Hunting Season

Snow covers the forest. In the thickets
Hangs the heavy breathing of runners in the drifts.
The drivers zealously shake the resonant
Winter air, together with the sound
Exhaling a light home brew vapor.
Soon shell shots rain out,
Crows caw at the forest's edge.
First blood
Paints the hands and hides,
The operation room's sheets,
The white funeral linens....

The campfire's blue smoke rises into a gray sky.
A mournful hunting meal: smoked meat,
Warmth under the tongue, conversations about matters.
A storm rises,
The hounds of wind drive in hordes of white flies
And hurl them into the trees.
They pack their things and return quickly to an ordinary
Life, where the wind of time
Drives the souls of hunters to the line of death
And the wind of space lays down
On them the heaviness of an ordered world.

January, 1988

Nihilists

One form of nihilism is Plato's
When he, as Heidegger affirms,
Sees Existence having forgotten Being.
Another nihilism is the young man's,
For whom it is the same to spit at Being
And beings as he struts into a bar
Fingering the money in his pocket
And looks at the girls, making plans for the night,
And sitting down at a table
Discourses to the red-nosed around him
About the vanity of the world.
Still another is the nihilism of the poet
Who understands nothing sufficiently
But who worries about saying ever more.

July, 1987

Gamblers

They throw dice. The sun stares
Reproachfully and hides behind a jagged forest.
They do not see the sun, only the numbers,
Bet
Their knowledge, beliefs, consciences,
But never win.
Because there is nothing to win:
Who needs a foreign wisdom, beliefs?
And each has sufficient conscience...
But one comes
And casts his life on the drum:
Drum drum—the highest
Powers, *drum drum*—the lowest...
Until the tumbling dice
Show nothing.

December, 1988

Epiphanies

Sometimes, while bent over at the waist
At the right angle with respect to the wall
And harmoniously resounding
With — say — the furniture in the entrance hall,
You are suddenly aware
Of all the beauty of poetry and the world,
Warm streams of wisdom penetrate into stinking nooks
And begin to wash across the compressed
Silt of mechanical perceptions...

But will you really stand
Who knows how long this way
Holding the shoe waiting to be put on?

August, 1986

Advice to the Adept

Take some spirit, take as much as you can,
Mix it with gentlest ether
Flowing in your veins.
You will get a soul, which you will blow into substance.
Do it the way God does it—bravely and obliviously.
Then before your eyes a body will be born.
It will be more radiant than Pygmalion's woman.
But you have to lay it
Without compassion on the table and embalm it—
Life will disappear on its own—
Lay it into a coffin or sarcophagus
And lower it into a grave.
Then build a monument,
Which will be the title of a poem
Or the first line.

November, 1987

Spider

My heart—like a tuft
In the spider's belly.
Unwinding a resilient thread
From which I knit a net around you, my love,
And sit cowering in the brambles of my body
Until the rapacious retinas of my eyes quiver,
Touched by the thing I desire,
And while attacking my victim I realize that
It's only my own shadow.

November, 1987

Two Ways

There is the way of the sage and the warrior. The first
Leads down viscous and erroneous
Quagmires of the knowledge of truth
Endlessly litigated with gods.
When a decision is made to act
It is unclear who determines the way—
The sage or the merchant.
Sometimes clearly it is the merchant who chooses
In the name or bearing the name of the sage.
Where this path leads,
I do not know.

The warrior's way stretches through gardens of virtue,
On the blade of a single truth.
It is the way of will and not of knowledge.
The soul is not soiled on it,
There is no need to choose.
Where this road leads
I do not know as well.
Both disappear behind the cemetery hill.

There is also the way of the merchant,
Which we are following.

June, 1987

Bookish Vengeance

They rode into our village
Creaking with rusted helmet visors
Led by a gray-bearded old man in whose eyes
Were endless faith, hunger and emptiness
And on whose chest was hammered
The sign of Saturn. They rode to avenge
Some offense against their god.
They killed a few boys and sick people
Who tried to resist. The men were gone.
They stopped beneath an oak tree
To catch their breaths. Then spread through the village.

The cries of women fill the cupola of heaven,
The impotent anger of old men
Penetrates stones,
Eats the eyes of the gods,
Crumbles the corners of the sky.
Terror and hopelessness flood
Through the cottage windows.
Beneath the sacred tree
Grows a mountain of infants.
Small bloody bodies
Shudder in the powdered snow.
Thin red streams flow to the middle of the street.

Someone tried to call out to gods, but the earth opened
And swallowed him. Someone
Tried to speak but from his mouth
Came only the yelping of dogs.
They sat where they stood, held their heads
On hands of stone.
In the splinters of their world
As an unfamiliar wind blew through the cracks of the sky.
The rising sun, lighting the road for the fugitives,

ZDANYS

Found all the people of the village frozen
To tombstones of ice.

And the boys outside the village dug a long trench
Poking clumps of earth with spears.
Girls cooked food in their homes, concentrating on their work
As if fulfilling some ritual,
And the youngest children
Chased dogs away from the corpses with sticks
And sang something about the sun.

May, 1983

Ave, Caesar

My poor body. Joints
Are sprained, skin hacked by rods, fetters
Cut deeply into muscles. But this suffering is ending.
We are already being driven into the pen where hungry lions
And tigers will soon be loosed. They will tear us apart,
Will set our souls free like doves into the azure sky.
Ave, Caesar, hail god, from God
(As the small Jew said,
Our fire-eyed apostle) having received the power
To judge and sentence us to death. I was born
In Thessaly, that's why I have some skill in understanding
Hidden matters. I entered that sect of new-believers
Out of despair, thinking
That Christ's truth might take root in the world
And would manage to change it for the better. At least reading
Their ancient writings such a hope unfolds.
In any event, I really had nothing to choose. For now they are
Growing, need deaths and executions, martyrs and torturers,
Right ones and wrong ones, whom they will create
With your hands, Caesar, in the eyes of this crowd,
Which will slowly be brutalized along with your lions.
I have never before felt so alone
And so free. Kingdoms or congregations of believers—
Only a sheet hiding a man's great loneliness
In the context of being. The first says it defends the body,
The second—the soul, but a man's life must
Conform to being's form. All of our
Spiritual and intellectual strengths strive to recognize it,
Strive to come to believe, persuade ourselves,
That the form revealed to us is real...
I am not convinced, though this is not disbelief,
That the form of being is the same for all people
And that you and I, Caesar, have been fated the same road.
I simply comprehend time, which has passed since my baptism,
As my conscious "yes," that's why I am freeing myself

ZDANYS

From my body, whose customs are abundantly clear.
We are both tied together, Caesar, only you are at the other
End of the chain. My throat will be torn open
By the beasts of the sun god, the Mithra-faced lion
With the golden flaming mane.
And our Son of Man
Sooner or later will have to put on that face.
And you, Caesar, walk down the path marked by your gods
To sunset. Your gods are weakening
And the form of your being is fading. Our deaths
Suck out the juices of your life and if you consider
What to do next as you watch my body being torn apart,
The Empire will linger for a time and if
Your head spins along with the mob
As our intestines are flung about,
The people of the new religion will grab not only the form
Of my death but the form
Of your life as well and with them will strain the world's
Powers, will direct them to their own mills, their own sails.
We are both alone, while the form of being
Is equally hidden from us both. Leaving
You always doubt
What you had heard while alive because you don't know
The reasons why you were being told it.
That's why I think that I have to forgive you everything
And at the same time expect your forgiveness
Because death itself is forgiveness. Ave, Caesar,
Moriturus te salutat.

September, 1988

The Labyrinth

Suddenly the sharp air cuts into my nostrils,
The wind's cold shags stick to my body
And light blazes into my eyes like smelted
Metal. Raising the sword
Of my voice I stand in the doorway
On the other bank of the troubled brook.
A tepid current carries away the last of the blood
Washed from my body,
Mine, which does not as yet possess itself —
A small god in the world's flowering spider web
Raising his weapon to the smiling sky...

Then gray landscapes flock through the gates of my eyes,
Cities and people, rooms and words,
Like bees carrying nectar to a giant hive,
Which I will later identify with myself,
    later when it
Is full and most foreign to me.
(To a wooden frame, a regular wax construction?)
The cliches of thought and standards of conduct
Begin pushing through the five gates
Exiling emotions to undergrounds
According to the tenets of the school of perfidy and struggle...
But instead of a clear calculated world
Each one finds here his own labyrinth,
Intricate, three-storied. A woman in a black cowl
Meets you at the entrance and behaves
As if not knowing how we intend to live
    or not wanting to know.

Stairs up and down.
Light diffusing from the top floor —
A white lily surrounded by unearthly music,
Many white rooms, radiant corridors,
Transparent blissful incoherence —
The land of gods.

Prosperity decolors the soul, moths of light
Hack the dowry of merits.
The core of memory melts and its grave
Powers waste away like an unused organ.

But it is unclear who is chasing us past many stairs,
Keeps us from rising,
Perhaps regret for the dust of this bi-fold floor,
Dismal repetitive experiences,
Perhaps dark longings
Enveloped in cunning explanations.
Love for the labyrinth's second floor has many faces. It is
Not only love for the sensations and the world they reflect,
It is everything that takes a person away from himself
And in him gives himself to the community
And in that way seals up the basement's solid ceiling
That protects us from darkness and destruction.
That's why love for a person, nation, mankind,
Education, church, society, art
In essence is ambiguous and (unfiltered through the self)
Does not differ from accumulation of wealth or physical pleasures.
It is the obscure dead end streets of the solar plexus
Where each wanders among familiar decorations:
Through the unfinished shrine, puppet theater, slaughterhouse,
The courthouse with ten thousand rooms.
(It may be that even after death
These images will persecute us, having managed
To bite off at least a tiny sliver of the dead's time
With their demonic jaws
And stand in a lewd shape of reality
In front of a decaying consciousness.) We
Do not live badly in that region of the waist,
Comfortably, mechanically, sedentarily.
Thought disturbed our peace for a long time,
Until it was castrated by logic, which convinced us
That the purpose of thought was conclusions,
Definitions,
And not the awareness

That thought must be of high quality.
And if we inquire what that means
They point out divine technology.
Is that not why among those who can't overstep conclusions
Appeared so many self-intoxicating ones
Who still remember the lights of distant houses
Though they know only the artificial way, and to overcome it
Purchase tickets from death?
But it is not worth our while to pay attention
To the insignificant spoilage of decorations—seams,
Connections, cardboard leaves
Hiding holes to the bottom and top floors,
It's not necessary to listen to those who talk
About the world, of which we all are part,
It's not necessary to vindicate the erring.

I quickly pass the stairs to the basement,
    on shaking legs
Creep near the holes beckoning me to jump
Down into the soft and comfortable darkness.
Gods of the five senses live there
Ruled by the sixth, who is like a ball
Among coins with two different halves.
    The pleasures of sensation
Are linked to the body only on the middle floor.
And elsewhere their movement is incomprehensible,
    but as concretely felt
As music. Between the perception of love, death,
And beauty. Between paralyzing terror
And the Minotaur's intoxicating smell.
If only the ball of yarn
Of the black-robed teen, filled with visions
Of motherhood, would not lead us into the light,
Into the world.

    Where we later try to perform
Excerpts from our journeys,
But disillusioned realize

That the plays are not that good,
That a personage unexpectedly appears in each of them,
Deus ex machina announcing himself somewhere
Up high and poisoning our performance with his grumbling,
That on this floor there are not only joys but also duties
And the joys of duty are the very greatest,
Especially if they are changed to blessings.
    We imagine here
Acting out the mysteries of the top floor,
About which we comprehend little.
    Listening to the emptiness
We create rituals and perform them sincerely,
Believing that, according to the laws of magic,
Their orgasms or catharses
Will image us into brighter and more eternal existence.
Longing for the sense of being
Governs us more firmly than desire for life or love.
(But perhaps the underground and the top is the same floor,
Changing lighting and decorations,
The way day changes night?)
    The thread
Always brings us back to the corpse
From which power quietly gushes, fills our
Rituals and daily routines, grants the strength
To overcome one more turn of the wheel.
    And the symbol of the center
Pulses ever stronger, rises to the light
Like a lily's black bud from the silty bottom.
And you see how all the labyrinth's floors
Stretch their erring galleries into a blossom.
And you follow the thread and see the exit
After a thousand years or tries,
In emptiness and loneliness,
In the endless corridors of time,
Where only the voiceless images of predecessors
Stare into your eyes.

November, 1986

II

on a dream's face
on a muggy June night
the plaster stiffens

Apocrypha

On the road to Golgotha
Ahasuerus is still chasing the man with a cross
Away from his home while in Jerusalem's customs house
Scripture's decoders already compose secret documents,
Prepare visas for the apostles,
Study life in the diaspora, strengthen
The net of agents in Rome and in the provinces.
It is essential to evaluate correctly
The Grecian spirit, the hunger in their souls,
Their dreams, repeating for millennia.
(A man is nailed to a cross.)
The world is brutal and old. Ships of Gnosis
Abandon the exhausted civilization
And spread across the Mediterranean Sea, penetrate
Islands and seaside ports.
Reconnaissance multiplies the apocrypha
About the human nature of god.
(Guards cast lots for his cloak.)
Wise men consider the game plan
And that, which is outside the game,
Remains for the condemned,
Remains for travelers on this earth, leaving
Meekly one by one, because theirs is the kingdom of death.
A few influential
Foremen have plastic surgery.
The stone removed by the builders
Is mentioned ever more often.
Candidacies of martyrs are considered.
In the beginning was Logos.

November, 1983

ZDANYS

Court Case

Through the lilac bush, the thujas and shabby acacias,
I glanced at the world of nature
And discovered that it is good.
My body, the grass, the cracked pears,
Autumn apples and summer cherries...
It really is good, that's why my...
And only later did I see God
In the bush filled with sunset
And He demanded I return His world to Him.
And that's why we're in court now.
The case has already reached the highest tribunal.
Everyone testifies on my behalf.
Light says: who would see me if not you?
Air says: who would breathe me if not you?
Earth says: who would walk on me if not you?
But He presents some ancient papers
That I do not know how to read.
And there is less and less time, and there, on the other side,
Other laws may be more valid...

December, 1989

The Jinn

> All those who distort truth and do harm
> to the teachings of the Church are
> the Samarian Simon Magus' apostles and disciples...
> In truth—they do not carry before them the
> name of Jesus Christ but in all manner
> teach us Simon's godlessness...
> pouring into the ears of the listener the
> Great Serpent's (Satan's), the primal apostate's, poison.
> St. Iranaeus, Adversus Haeresus

You are mistaken, Samaelis, blind god.

Once we rode out on camels to Nag Hammadi—
I, Muhammad Ali al-Sammam, and my brothers—
To bring fertilizing silt back to our fields.
While digging it we found a clay jug sealed tightly with a cork.
I was seized by fear. I thought a jinn was in it.
But the hope to find gold lifted my pick.
Beneath the scattered fragments were thirteen papyrus
Books we brought home and piled near the hearth
In my life, mute, dreary, and stifling as the earth.
Perhaps only metabolism is quicker there: women
Sometimes used leaves for kindling. That's how everything
Would have ended but a few weeks later Allah allowed
My brothers and me to sneak up on our father's murderer,
One Ahmed Ismail, and we then released
His despicable soul from his body, let it loose to the winds,
Chopped off his feet, hands, afterwards tore out his heart
And divided it with a knife and ate it raw the way we were taught
By the rites of vengeance, buried what remained under a juniper.
We were young and hot, were not afraid to kill and die.
The police began questioning us and we had to hide
Those books at a neighbor's. And they began to rise slowly
Into the dim light of minds where they were burned in the spirit's flames,
Washed by the water of souls, this extract was carried by blood...

Whether we found gold or freed a jinn
I didn't know for a long time and, of course, felt sorry
About the gold, which I would have raked in for them,
But later I started to connect it all to my father's
And his murderer's deaths. Even though that spring
A great world war had ended, having spilled oceans of blood,
Having released winds of souls. Finding me, various
People asked how and when we had found those books.
In exchange, I asked what was written in them...
And at last understood that the murderer of the tribe's stepfather,
Dying then on the cross, was the son of the Highest Deity.
Intoxicated by his death the Archons lost their vigilance
Because, it appears, death always worked to calm them—
The spring of danger disappears: the soul leaving the world
Carries light there where their understanding does not reach.
So through the open door wisdom flooded our hearts,
And the Archons' vassals had to labor hard
Until they tangled truth, distorted his words and origin,
Created clever writings and hierarchies supported by force,
So that in the hearths of existence books and people would quietly burn,
And there would be only one truth, which they called truth.
But I still don't know who, having filled the jug
With blood, gave it to the thirsty spirits of the desert to guard,
Whose will he was fulfilling, and who suggested the way...
Who am I, after all, and whose hand governs me,
How much free will do I have, how much truth am I allowed to know?—
I ask myself all the more often and all the more often forget to pray.

You are mistaken, Samaelis, god of the blind.

Explanation
I received a handwritten translation into English
Of this text from a Portuguese who called himself
A millionaire, though he made a living as a journalist
And looked a great deal like an antiques dealer.
I remember how, after the third gin and tonic in the littered
Bar in Seville, he began fumbling through his pockets (the TV
Was broadcasting a corrida, the one in which the famous matador

Died in the spring of 1992), until he finally found a soiled
And tightly folded piece of paper and gave it to me saying
That he had gotten the translation from an Arab friend of his
Who worked in some museum in Cairo.
But I have no doubt whatsoever that this is an apocrypha
Even though real people and events are mentioned in it.
Muhammad Ali, a Moslem, reasons
Like a primer Gnostic who, after "A Thousand and One Nights,"
Had read some version of the "Apochryphon of John."
But I think this story is worthy of publication, so our
Reader would see by what sort of bloody sacrifices
The sweet-talking spirits of hell vomit
From their jaws those clever error-filled heresies. I added
The epigraph myself, because I think it especially fits
Publication of the text in Lithuania. Its first line
Is a quotation from one of the Nag Hammadi books,
"The Essence of the Archons," and the last from "About the
    Origin of the World."
In both instances it is the response of the Absolute to him who said:
"I am god and there is no other god before me!"

November, 1994

The Peaceable Song

I

We rode through the black tunnel of night
By two, together with ourselves, warrior.
Meanings are confused, systems of signs imperfect,
Allusions collapse with every
Brick that's moved. The father of things is ailing.
Those two armies... Darkness against darkness.
Military operations give birth to ideologies
And corpses. Stations along the way flash by.
From the platform the noisy hymn of some sect
Tumbling in through the window, tears at the car's silence—
Old longing of existence forcing its way past teeth of bone—
And there is nowhere to hide from a holy life,
From conversion, from recovery, from verbalized goodness,
Which gnaws out the eyes, eats away consciousness,
Sucks the green blood out of leaves, the red from veins,
The white from testicles, lymph canals, even washes
Milk from breasts and settles in powder
At the bottom of consciousness.
If there is no harmony within you...
You understand who the architect of these stations is.
You understand it on your own.
I am not god, am not more sensible than you
And do not want to force you to live with my illusions.
I am only the train's engineer, whose entire wisdom—
The traffic schedule and a few well-worn handles.
I can share with you only reluctance,
Incertitude and hesitation. The architect
Offers everyone the same station interior
But the spirit to understand truth is given to us
By God. We cannot pass it
One to another. We give each other
Only truths themselves. And perhaps are
Able to recount in some unclear way

Along which road we were able to reach them.
So many worlds have perished, which had their distinctive wisdom.
Only crumbs remain for us: random texts
With contexts, their errors, lacunae,
Dead languages, which no one knows,
But they decipher, speculate, reconstruct, interpret,
Render their thoughts in the words of a completely different time,
Give them to builders, who quickly cement them into
Their own ideologies, imputing their own dimensions
To history, adulterating the causes of events,
Appropriating time in order to usurp a space—
The earth of souls and mother earth...
And you want to fight for them?

II

Two armies lining the path to the abode
Of your soul, one against the other, in both
Familiar faces.
It is your struggle, warrior, your holy war
From which you have nowhere to retreat.
Just do not ask me about reality and reflection,
I do not know, you will know when you fight.
Now put down your fruitless contemplations.
Watch how the sun rises mornings, how the tree's
Leaf unfolds, how the fledgling bird hammers its way
Into the place suddenly opened for it by the one just dead.
Do not allow the hydra of words and images to wind around
Your sturdy muscles and the battle ready bow.
Beyond her open jaws gape endless
Wildernesses of demons, their armies wait
Until you forget the moment, until you hold them
As "real," until you neglect God's world
And march trustingly into the Architect's domain
Like a sacrifice festooned with flowers...
Essences are clouded, systems of signs imperfect,
Reality like a single two-sided mirror stretching all around,
With the Architect's so-called holy books,

Where everything is tangled, distorted and doubled,
That is why I have told you not to mislead your mind in them.
The road to God is simple and straight
Like the battle for which you have been born.
Everything grows clearer when we begin to act correctly.
But we set many snares for ourselves
With passions and considerations,
And the clever ones set snares
Attempting to explain the harmony they never knew.
They entangle the warrior's consciousness, suck out his power,
Cast his gaze down to a tangle of sinews.
Two-faced heads of communities, threatening and wronged,
Extend hands not their own into your conscience
According to the Architect's instructions.
But you have your own battle—two armies
Lining the path to your soul's abode.
Look what expanses chaos has usurped,
How wide is death's dominion!
God has destined you to struggle and overcome.
If you are not trapped in the scene painter's snares,
If you do not become their friend or foe,
If you do not begin to count what you can win here
In this emptiness and wait for the fruits
Of the tree nourished by the sap of a different causality.

III

The father of things is ailing. An odd peace
Fetters the heart. The phalanxes of death draw near. Forgive
Me these words, warrior, forgive my refusal
To reconcile both worlds—impotence
Surpasses my soul and will,
I am only the train's engineer and the rails were laid long ago
And the switch men always specify the way.
That's why it's not worth fighting for nothing
Without winning the battle inside yourself,
Without conquering the ground that would nurture the action.
There is much knowledge in the world but we each

Must begin this battle anew: sooner or later
Knowledge negates itself.
Forgive me if I speak without knowing—
Some time ago I took on this speaker's destiny
And now it's too late to withdraw.
But I lack the strength to go on.
The hope that you will do this for me remains.
Ahead everything is strange, confused, suspicious,
There are many truths and many similarities to truth.
The hero is born alone and alone leaves the battlefield
And creates his own reward.
Windmills truly can look like four-armed
Monsters. And the opposite. But
Mistakes are never forgiven.
Because there is no person in the chain of causes
And consequences, no one to offer forgiveness. The action,
External and internal, means the same and
Both are followed by doubled consequences.
If you fight for those who want to force you to fight
Their war, you will accumulate only your own faults and merits,
Which you will not return to them.
Though they promise you protection in this world
And after death... I don't know.
I'm not sure. I am beset by doubts,
Which I pass on to you. It is my only
Treasure, my only wisdom.

October, 1992

About Starlings Ten Years Later

Remember—I wrote about a starling
Whistling outside the window? And now
Every spring it repeats itself
Even though the birdhouse is caked with droppings.
I too have written a sufficient number of lines,
And besides, the community's ear has changed.
It began to seem to me that the bird,
Singing the same songs all these years,
Knows how to sing without annoying,
But the poet, setting out the same words
In ever different ways, bores
Even himself. Besides, I have a home,
Became a father long ago—
So what should I call out for,
To what should I surrender my heart?
Nature falls asleep in my veins, spring
Becomes ever more like winter.
Our songs are different—his soars away
But mine lags behind the meaning
That the Creator gives to his feathered ones.

July, 1994

Fisherman

In the box of my skull thoughts wriggle like worms,
the surface of the lake is still
as the mirror of the soul.
The fisherman's clumsy fingers grope for the worm,
mount it on the hook, the fishing line stretches on the water.
Shoulders crouch beneath a mantle of ermine.
What fish, what fish will he catch now?
Long as a spindle? Flat as a full moon?
Full of life's life? Death's death?
A fishing line tangling eel?
A hierarchical carp?
IXTHYS? Or perhaps nothing?
Perhaps his worms are not attractive
to the fish in this lake? Perhaps its mirror-like surface
has frozen to ice, and ice turned to steel,
separating these two worlds with a crust of death?
And no savior will come. From where would he come?
And who would he be—man, fish, or perhaps
a bolt of lightning, perhaps a puff of the spring wind?
The float dips under water. Ah, yes,
it's a poem's roach fish, a box,
the swarming worms of words.

March, 1997

I Don't Worry About Culture

The wild grape ends its choking
growth over the unpruned plum
whose branches will be broken by ripening fruits,
two young oaks already smother the cherries
in the garden corner. Everything is grown by natura,
it spreads within me, sending its vines through
my body's openings, winding around my soul
like potato sprouts in a dark cellar becoming
something else, distorting ordinary
instincts and physiological needs.
The cherries grow smaller, sour, fruits
and consequences turn bitter. Spoiled wine
quickly carries me to black oblivion.

July, 1998

Rodeo

I jump on the bull's back, the gates open,
and the two of us break out into the arena of stinking sand
which has drunk its share of sweat, nose foam and blood,
and begin our reckless dance. Two currents
intersect, two wills grapple furiously,
and the result of their struggle—only a time span,
so contemptibly small in the presence of eternity.
                Falling
down, I manage to see a prudent
old man billowing on a bull's back
to the west, down river, down wind, the way time flows,
space and fluids gush through the arteries of the living.

February, 1999

Tidal Zone

She withdraws following the governing moon
with the waters and ghosts, with her creatures,
leaving behind the dark brown heads of stones
to stick up out of the shallows, coarse,
silt-covered footbridges among them,
clear puddles with seashells
and amphora shards sowing their bottoms, with
small fish brisk as thoughts, crustaceans slow
as contemplation, husks of bodies and souls
that for a moment connect the eye with the sun's light.

No man's land, unstable, but of stable rhythm,
a heron jumping from stone to stone
investigates the bottom with its beak and eyes,
the reefs' teeth hold back the great waters.

After the moon I drag the cloak of consciousness
and after the sun I try
to close up an image in a form.

June, 2000

The Top

We decided it was time to chop down
the early plum tree, in the summer giving us
a large harvest that no one needed.
Half of it was overrun by a wild grapevine
and a few of its branches were already drying.
But in the fall it unexpectedly loaded
with buds and exploded into white blossoms
right in the face of our somber thoughts.
Mad juices in the old trunk's veins,
the top like a bride's headdress
in the autumn rain.

October, 1998

Home

Long walked upon paths retrieve the feet,
Things in memory renew the imprints of fingers.
Your comfortable body and wise soul...
The pillows of recollections slowly wane
Beneath my hands, shadows
Slip out from between us like secret
Love letters from long unread books,
Smiles close, and the reservoirs of eyes, from which
I just emerged, overgrow with weeds.
Fingers move across the familiar keyboard
And make mistakes as if touching the one
Across which they wandered all month.

November, 1994

Night Bather

The heart is restless, the fragrant spring air
full of noise. She walks
through the garden gate and turns down the path
across the meadow, dressed severely, the only place
uncovered that small spot where the neck flows into the back,
face powdered, lips distinctly colored, eyebrows
thinly plucked, walks in small steps
at the edges of yards, hides in the alder grove,
appears again near the silvered brook where it
pours itself into the pond. The same moonlight is in her eyes.
She husks herself from the severe dress—her white skin
is even paler against the wall of shadows—
and wades into the water which, uneasily rippling,
pulls away from the foreign and unfamiliar body,
from the strong smell of perfume and perspiration, she bends
and two small snakes wind downstream—the red
of her lips and the pale dust of her powder,
the etheric oils of her perfume, everything
to the very foam of her body, to the disquiet of her soul.

Moonlight's silver is in the eye of the watching deer,
the intoxicating animal smell in the hounds' nostrils....

I still remember her raised arm
against a background of blossoming cherries, the outline
of her fingers above an embroidered sleeve, a few petals
in her hair of the color of raven,
waving farewell.

June, 2000

Apples

In trolley number 5 on the last seat
Next to a dozing old man from Gerontion,
A bag of red apples on my lap. Not for Paris,
Not for Alexander, but for my children, my family.
Unwittingly the apples of my breasts pulsate with juices.
The young man near the door across from me on the step,
Fixing his gaze on the apples, the juices, the reward,
Gathers, it seems, something from the shadows of his soul.
Between his legs the root of life begins to grow,
The uncontrollable horn stiffens, and he reddens in shame.
The old man, seeing that, wakes and begins to chuckle.
The young man, flustered, gets off at the first stop.
The old man continues chuckling, my body grows numb,
Its juices begin to rage. I try to get out
At the next stop but my forgotten bag
Falls off my lap and the red apples spill out.
Undelivered reward. The old man laughs
And begins picking up the apples. Not for Alexander,
Not for Paris, but for my children, my family. I get off.
Back past the old men's voices, past the faces of Achivi.
May the gods send him his soul's most beautiful woman.

December, 1996

Hades Kidnaps Persephone

A fly bangs against the glass searching for a warm crack,
A saw's teeth greedily cling to wood,
Hades seizes Persephone in his arms, panting
Heavily he lifts her fat bottom off the ground,
The black harnessed steeds wait
And dig the soil with their hooves, fat-thighed nymphs
Wring their hands, bang against the cool air, weep
Like saws. Carelessly flowing
Time congeals into forms, life into its signs,
Water into flakes of snow, experiences into allusions
With which poetry is strewn, describing the bright landscape
Of life, diffusing the scent of Hades.

October, 1998

Aging Gods

Shortness of breath constricts my chest with my first step.
I shamefully hide my tenacious radiant rays
Behind a fluffy screen of clouds.
Branches leap back into arms, the trunk rounds back into a waist
Gracefully enclosed in the firm half-circles of maidenly hips.
The coarse bark is replaced by smooth skin,
Leaves tatter into hair and stick to the head and underbelly,
Mounds of breasts rise, shoulders curve,
Legs move ever more slowly
Until they finally stop. The chest heaves quickly.
The scene becoming image: the persecutor has vanished.
I throw the laurel wreath under her feet—the contest is over,
Victories confer no joy, flutes fall silent,
Bend and break loose from lips.
Her perfect proportions captivate everybody.
The world's image fades on the screen.

August, 1998

St. Elizabeth's Hospital

> *Our dynasty came because of a great sensibility.*
> Ezra Pound, Canto 85

Across the Anacostia River, among the trees,
St. Elizabeth slices a round cake
with a long shining knife and politely serves it
to the students of the poetry t-group waiting in line.
Their arms are bound along their bodies to the elbow,
their eyes as round as a cake sun,
they stretch oddly as they eat: it is the destiny
of poetry to repair consciousnesses and worlds. Suddenly
a telephone rings, calling for St. Elizabeth,
she hands over the knife and asks me to continue slicing.
As the long blade travels from one hand to the other
the sun bounces off and flashes in their eyes
chopping up their roundness like the knife
the cake. The world splinters
into myriad fragments and for a moment
congeals before crumbling. I

  Our dynasty came
    because of a great sensibility.
  After all the pavilions of our palaces
    I now look through John Howard's window.
  From the shadow of leafless trees
    into the new age across the river.
  Our minds were somewhere else
    when the gates opened.
  Our dynasty rested upon a strict hierarchy
    contemplating beauty.
  The walls dissolved years ago
    as I listened to forbidden places.
  Our dynasty established order in poetry
    and gushed through the edges of form.
  Inner voice? Each of us got many

           inner voices. Which would you like to hear?
Our dynasty was hospitalized
      because of its great faith.
The new world injected us with tranquilizers
      and our consciousnesses turned to wood.
St. Elizabeth took us into her care
      and love dissolved our will.
The founders of the world of equal values
      took to healing us with our own poetry.
The inexhaustible milk in St. Elizabeth's pitcher
      undermined the hierarchies' foundations.

stick the blade into the cake, splintered
reality holds together, an odd hope that already shone
through the cracks seals over. The poetry
t-group students meekly lower their eyes.
The balsam of words oozes through the cell walls—
glue of things and consciousnesses with bandaged arms—
the metal taste in my mouth is changed by the sweetness of cake,
returning us to harmonies, opening up
memory's roads to nowhere.

Parts of a poetry fusion made by Craig Czury from the works of contemporary patients at St. E's Hospital are used in this text.

                                                                    August, 1999

The Barbarian

And they lived long enough to see us.
They saw our pure divine sun,
Our pale moon and unrestrained fire,
Our heavy oak battering rams, spiked cudgels,
Primordially flowing blood, savage death.

Ruins of palaces, shrines,
Trisyllabic feet, strewn incoherently,
Scattered iambs.
I cannot understand their subtle allusions,
Anemic snares, winding around a warrior's thoughts
And sucking their healthy blood. They
Do not reach my sensations, do not stimulate any emotions,
Only disgust for their sweet weakness and boredom.

I confess poetry, the power rendered to words.
I, a barbarian bard, a bit weary
Of the spilling of blood, ruins and ashes.
I know—this power grows from the truth
Like an oak from red clay,
From our nature, from not thinking, not naming,
From the desire to influence but not understand,
To call forth the rain, silence the elements,
Tame epidemics...
Because truth belongs to the gods, not to the minds of poets...

And afterwards,
The furies abated and with consciousness softened
I try to tell stories about the exploits of war,
And ever more peaceful things, gathering feet,
Scattered in the grass whose roots are the first
To capture the fecundity of ashes and blood.

July, 1997

Suburban Pine Forests

They begin there, where orderly
Or dirty city streets end, and sometimes
They penetrate into the depths of our settlements
And encroach upon our cultivated parks.
Saturated with dust, gasoline fumes and soot,
Littered and trampled, carefully
Washed with acid rainfalls and snows
They purify the air.
The city attacks them fiercely on all sides,
Cuts them off from the forests, closes them up
In fortress cauldrons, strives to destroy them
Or at least change them into parks.
They keep on patiently, growing mosses,
Scanty underbrush, building fortifications of bushes
According to their obedient and patient military knowledge.
Consistently, here and there appear mountains of refuse,
Secretly discarded by the dump trucks of the self-improving city.
Corpses are discovered—victims of violence, sad
Hangers or other suicides.
The gloomy outcomes of varied conflicts, oppressively
Unfolding in the city's boxes—the dust of aging bodies,
Fumes of sick thoughts, the soot of souls, the refuse
Of uniformed imaginings, discarded into the unconscious,
Where drunkards roam, collectors of empty bottles,
Where maniacs primed by their secret desires wander,
Where inquisitive children prowl, and sometimes
Lovers come by chance or other residents swollen with passion,
Having nowhere else to share their stiff cravings.
The pine forests accept all that quietly, bear no testimony, do not resist,
Just gently purify the air and constantly look for the chance
To return the trash and corpses to the city
Publicly, indifferently and shockingly,
Like our own unconscious—all those insects
Swarming in the boxes of the city,
Thinking, loving, quarreling—attacking
It with their streets, houses and cemeteries.

March, 1997

Unexpected Guests

It is to you, unexpected guests,
Connected only by semantic features,
That I dedicate these poor lines.

You did not manage to outstay here,
Take over our ideas and texts
And change anything with your will.

You, illegitimate child of fairy tales,
Born in secret, were released into the river in a box
Packed together with the most beautiful things.

You, invalid, wounded while forcing
Your way through the gates of this world,
Were left by your lawful parents in the room's box
As they ran away through the window into night
On a flowing river of darkness,
Carrying off only things.

And you, stranger,
Discovered in a rubbish heap, in a polyethylene bag,
With an umbilical cord wrapped round your neck...

You all returned there from where you chanced to come
Or wandered off to some other place. And if it came to be
That we are destined to take this excursion only once
It would be difficult to reconcile
The absurdity.

December, 1995

The Necessities of a Diary

Because afterwards everything intertwines, merges,
Great imaginings
Crumble into a thousand pieces, tiny homunculi,
Watching your dreams and meditations.
Though calendar time never coincides
With a soul's history, it alone
Links it with "history."
So if you can find no other way
To protect yourselves against diminishment,
Ever-shorter years, blunting sensations, longing,
From that which is given too late, when desire
Comes only from habit, remembering past desires,
And you are not even sure if you ever really
Had them, or if they were in fact
The rats of mangy consciousness
Spawned by poor reading and banal ideas, then
You open your diary
And there read your old lies
To yourself, and connecting them to world history
Create new truths, great imaginings.
Because there are as many minds
As sands on the ocean's shore—they
Are carried by the wind and tossed by the waves
And do not know why.

February, 1998

Evening Music

A tranquil thicket of alders
Near the black-bottomed brook, a rotted
Bench, a trash can. An old man
From the shelter comes here evenings, looks around,
Pulls out a harmonica
And plays "God save the king!"

March, 1983

Sunfish Heads

Sunfish lose their heads
Before Christmas Eve,
Their bodies lie on a dish on the table,
Dejectedly pressed together,
And cannot speak, have no means to.
At the same time their mouths slide from a damp
Slimy plastic bag
And fall into the snow. A jay
Lands on a nearby tree
From an empty sky.

And it's not clear who will sow their milt,
Who will fertilize their roe,
Who will carry our souls
To paradises or embryos...

24/12/1995

The Fisher Hawk

Water carries away sadness,
Air takes away desire.
The grass on the stream bed is like my rambling dreams.
The reflection of a bird floats past on the surface.
The season of blossoming, hunger.
Fish jump from the water into another
World and grab winged insects,
The fish hawk
Lies in wait for them on the fragrant air.
I walk out into there:
Rambling dreams, swaying, billowing...
To look for food?

May, 1997

Nasturtium

I remember them growing in the gardens of my childhood
Beneath rotting and unclean windows—
Frog-green leaves, slender shoots,
Stinking, as if diseased blossoms—
Seeming to coil from an unknown, strange world
That was not yet within me,
That revealed itself shyly in accidental signs.
Having shed their blossoms, they shamefully
Knotted together
Amazingly ugly bubbles
And closed up their seeds in them—
Creatures of that hell which was then only gathering up in me
And which later flourished
In flowers of evil.

December, 1995

A View of the Sea

I
At first I was surrounded by familiar ghosts, but when
Pricking my finger I paid my tribute of blood to the native spirits,
The dark and cold glass of the mirror came ajar,
Abruptly presented a view of the sea.
It spoke with clouds that slipped slowly across its face,
I do not know about what, but saw how its mood changed,
A smile fluttered here, fury foamed there.
I do not know what they said, what texts they exchanged,
Small or great, significant, inconsequential.
I did not know how to enter them or if there were others in that conversation,
The gray stones of Stella Mares, the Blessed Virgin's cathedral
With the ruins of other shrines around, measuring out
The hours with its bells, people's small houses by it...
I do not know what I can say to you, you who stopped
And looked at me quizzically as if summoned hastily
From the giddiness of your daily routine, my soul. List facts
Distorted by expression? Present expression
Without contents? Express feelings,
Formulate points of view, share
The resilient coolness of envisioned bodies?

II
The ether is full of meanings and perhaps the view of the blank wall
Would open other less deceptive landscapes
To him who knows how to wait.
But the wind raised white ruffles on the sea's leaden plane
Like an experienced lover shivers his partner's skin.
They rub across sensitive surfaces as if during the Fall.
The apple opens its memory with its stiff skin:
Two folders: a man's creations and behind them the foaming sea.
I open the first: cathedral, cottages, ruins;
I open the second: the sea But without ships or waves,
Without mermaids diving through its frothing curls.

I try to part its surface but memory
Tells me it does not know the way into this document.
I try to penetrate the system: strange signs,
Incomprehensible numbers and relationships. On what
Is this view founded: the eye's structure, the harmony of sensations?
On our kinship's or the programmer's contingencies?
What is known, experiences and perceptions?
Some sort of current
Flows suddenly into a shape open to it, employs it
And from somewhere lifts, as the sensations say, "truth". And still:
Two actions, switching on and switching off,
Which, if we believe the Bible kept in the cathedral,
Enclosed deceived original man with temporality when he,
Able to choose the fruit of immortality,
Took instead from his partner's hand the programmed apple...
And now we can believe whatever we want.
Existence is established hermetically. I close
The sea's file and folders.
Switch off the power.

III
I always wade into that same sea:
Beneath my feet my homeland's sand or the stones of a foreign shore,
Cold water cuddles me like a succubus,
The organs of thinking shrivel, the tentacles of dreams.
But I am always someone other,
Carried away, floated off, encrusted with shells
Engraved with the runes of strangest experience.
I feel how her flexible fingers open me:
The folders of sensations joined to the files of memories,
Accompanied by onomatopoetic interjections...
The touches of the wind, the tickling seagrasses, leaves.
And all this, just thoughts, meanings, words.
I would like to answer her, but—how?
Strike up a friendship with the denizens of her depths,
Which I do not see and whose language I do not know?
Sink into the truth of sensations, the essentiality of process,
Not managing and not reflecting,

Meeting on the other side of the body that unites them?..
Yes, she opened me, changed something and rendered it...
Ultimately I do not know what happened there, I must not have been present.
Then she closed me, daily routine with its names fell across
The labyrinth of my brain, words spilled from my lips.

IV
And you wade into that same sea,
Foambody beloved of the gods, paramour of swans,
Perfectly opened and radiant love!
God's invisible finger penetrates into you.
(Black? Yes, it most probably has to be
Black and lustrous as the surface of oil.)
Penetrates you, triumphantly leaves behind in you
Its liquid semblance,
Which can be deciphered only by the gentle memory of wombs,
Sorted out, apportioned in the matrices of its system...
And later they set the fruits, mature, grow strong,
Until it drips off a quill,
Opens like a flower not from this earth.
(Homer touched it with his blind man's finger,
Stesichorus went blind and then regained his sight.)
And so it is before you, Menelauses and Parises,
Step into her, penetrate her, decipher her substance!
Wander through her landscapes or conceive your
Children, become poets with souls that wade in the seas!
Our hermetic world foams with impenetrable
Texts, but there remained those who in the darkness of wombs
Could read life's
Letters and give birth again to its closed forms,
There remained elements and God, and nothing has changed
From the very time when nothing yet
Reflected the world.

October, 1994

Rolling

As a child I loved to play
in the street rolling a bicycle's
wheel rim with a stick.

A poor toy.
I remember that symbols
didn't interest me then.

Later, when I began to link
the straight and the circular
with images of time,
I contrived many meanings.

The world is round, and the individual,
stories and poetries.
Only history and truth are straight.

A woman is round
like wisdom, while the phallus is straight
like a slave's consciousness.

Perhaps that is why religions
propped up by history
so dislike and fear women.

I forgot this game long ago
though god keeps rolling
the world on the street of childhood
with something that looks like a phallus.

August, 1997

Ode to a Cracked Vase

O perfect bride of unfulfillment,
or overfilling, unbearable desire,
that cast us out of familiar orbits,
you stand proudly on the sideboard,
the barely visible crack turned to the wall.
And that's how souls sometimes don't withstand
passions that come on suddenly, desires
that fill their fragile amphoras.

Now, my dear, I will not discard you
just as we will not erase our memories,
even though you won't soak flowers nor willow
branches—you accept only dry bouquets,
beautiful as ever, shyly turning the crack
toward the wall you still try sometimes
to ignite the glance of some passing stranger
and quietly gather the hours' dust.

March, 1999

Delayed in Ephesus

Even before arriving
I was delayed there. Among newly-hewn marble,
In ancient time.
The mottled crowd of shadows was not at odds with my soul.
The theatrical repertoire and holiday rites,
Customs of thought and means of expression,
Childish games of love and undistorted passions suited me.
I was not close to them
Though did not feel more a stranger
Than I felt anywhere else,
So after many years, getting off the bus, one day
I set off down the main street that sloped to the library,
Along polished marble slabs pressed into the earth,
But right outside the temple of learning, eyes cast down,
I turned to the right, toward the amphitheater,
And found myself in the hetaera's quarter, where
To the city's ruler, the twenty-one-breasted, were
Offered living sacrifices:
Warm firm bodies on the cold and hard marble.
Cracks between slabs satiated with dreams,
Filled with pretentious images, which accompany
Such a simple act of impregnation. I remained there.
Having bought counterfeit drachmas with Odysseus's ship
From a gypsy woman's dirty hand, wanting to exchange them
Into noncounterfeit experiences. I remained there many years.
Because I had nowhere to go,
I wanted to speak, fortify myself with words, prove
Myself to the hetaeras who pushed me aside for lack of money.
Prove what? ... I don't know... I just wanted them.
Voices like battles of waves banging my ear drums.
I remained there many years.
I visited the forum, the amphitheater, the stadium, and baths,
Like everyone else I sent a slave to the public toilet,
In the center of which a band played,

To warm the marble slabs with his behind
Before I arrived. I listened to rumors
(There was no press then), slander and music.
(I was not often invited to symposiums.)
Yes, I had a tongue, lips, articulated sounds,
Knew several languages. But turned away from myself
I felt myself alone and inconsequential
In the ocean of sounds and shapes, words and sentences,
So one-sided, narrow.

The sea receded, unmoored
At least a few Renaissances and something opposite to them.
I joined them, leaving behind in Ephesus
My world view. I visited several peaceful harbors,
Uttered and wrote down many words,
Stayed in monasteries, hired myself out for various jobs,
Participated in banquets, taking goblets of wine
With two fingers and women's soft bodies
With both hands.
Until heavy satiety changed the pleasure of eating,
Wine clouded my vision, and women's bodies
With their smells and words destroyed my expectations
And left only emptiness in my body.
That life did not disperse my longing.
I lacked the will to walk down the path of the spirit
And I had nowhere else to go.
I was not attracted to this world of the present with its
Cultured lies, schizophrenias and complexes,
With its institutionalized religions and ideologies.
I was a stranger to it, even though I did not feel
More righteous, better, wiser than any other
Floating in the current. So I remained there.
Though ever more often I think I'll wait here
For my last day. Shadows, of course, will not carry out
The rites that separate my soul
From this world, will not accompany me to the other side.
Their world, this and that other, lives only in words.

ZDANYS

Like Sunday parks that many visit
But do not live in.
Yet my soul, alas, is absolutely real
Even though it always avoided any kind of reality.

August, 1995

III

*silent drowned people
in the clarifying river
traffic on the bridge*

The Tiller of the Soil

J.

The wind above those fields feels free.
She presses against the ground like a hen as it rages.
In the sky, larks and clouds, and heavenly bodies
higher still, but she is interested only in the field,

the yearly plowing, the black soil that accepts
the seed and returns the plants,
and beneath the black only clay and gravel
empty as the azure sky, untillable.

And the small cemetery outside the village, on a sandy hill.
Her most beautiful garden is there—flowers, lawns—
as she weeds she rises ever higher—almost
everyone here is familiar—relatives or neighbors.

Once, when burying a cousin, they dug a hole
alongside her mother's grave, splitting off an edge of her coffin,
and she jumped into the hole to look in through the crack,
to see how she felt there half a century later.

She was the same as when they buried her, only
black as a mummy, awaiting the last judgment
when she could reclaim her body, death's kingdom
is black as the soil, silent as the sky or sand.

May, 2002

Waking in Silence

Suddenly, silence,
a gloomy November morning,
a chainsaw slices it
near the boundaries of consciousness,
the soul's rooms muddled,
unmade beds, leftovers,
    (You heard the bell,
    the primrose in the silver
    silence? No, it just seemed so.)
empty bottles everywhere, Elpenor dead,
a hollow echo.
    There is nowhere to hurry to.

November, 2000

An Ordinary Meeting

I met her again tonight, straight chestnut
hair, white skin, a red dress
with an odd wooden frame from hips to ankles
hobbling her steps.
But nothing stopped her, she walked
through fences, hedges, walls, only once
turning her head she looked at me
indifferently and walked off through the yard,
straight through the den where a pighead
half lying against a spattered clay wall
stared at a gnawed son of man in the trough
as if he stared at himself.

Wait—I shouted—tell me what's happening
in these darknesses? She did not answer,
did not turn her head toward me
again.

April, 2002

Primavera

> *Midwinter spring is its own season*
> T. S. Eliot, "Little Gidding"

The early February sun shining
straight into the window woke
a dappled butterfly, the kind summers
are filled with. Its delicate wings
rustled the luminous curtains' snow
and it drank the sun with its feelers
in my room, where only a laurel bush
is eternally green in a plastic vase,
where only naked dreams slip out of the dark
and return again, having left only
a coal-like footprint on the paper's snow.
And where will you return: back to sleep,
having experienced the seductions of sun and life,
when real snowflakes spin outside the window,
or to the eternity, unfamiliar and strange,
that these words cautiously try to establish?

The next day it lay on its back again,
prosy, its legs entwined on its belly,
as if laid out by skilled providers
of ritual services. The sky was overcast,
colors faded.

February, 2002

Time to Write and Time to Change

It's time to write verse but also time to change the oil. I drove
more than 20,000 with the same. My car,
patiently and faithfully serving me, can no longer wait.
In the oily workshop among disassembled engine
parts, scattered tools, time presses my temples,
but the mechanic scrabbles, it's time to write verse
he talks on the phone, his pencil is a wrench, his paper
the oily can, my pencil's at home,
but if my faithful one falls apart, all of my allotted time
will burst into flame, bare breasted women on the walls,
it's time to write letters and time to change the customs
of mechanical style, my faithful one
is only a pile of metal, but all parts fit together,
my faithful one is not a woman but a machine,
my women, it's sad to say, are not so faithful,
there would be work for a mechanic in my soul too.
Finally a black stream stretches into the pail,
he changes the filter, signs in fresh oil.
A new time begins.

July, 2002

The Woman in Front of the Shop Window

She looked over the entire shop window, a beautiful
woman, still young, with a naked belly button
(that was the style), skin banal as a peach
in poetry. Spangles glittered in the window,
with which she liked to entice her prey—they alone
managed to give her glances any life—
metal sparkles
like brandished swords parrying against one another.
Hair, framing a carefully tended face,
asked not to be mussed,
and the stretched backs of her pants looked like new,
a luxurious gravesite or slaughterhouse, if you'd like,
for millions of those small tadpoles that invade her
with hope and faith, and suddenly
knock against a rubber wall, some sort
of deadly foam or something even more sophisticated
because their mission ends right here, in a common grave
(for if it was different it would be even sadder), I saw
her wandering down the corridors of a tangled labyrinth—
robber of an empty grave, overcoming
obstacles and strange monsters,
beautiful, safely imprisoned on a flickering screen.

June, 2002

An Ordinary Ascent

I washed my face with Castalian water
so His eye could look at me undisturbed
and began to climb the steep Parnassian hill.

I had no statue in my hands, no question on my lips.
I was met by ruins. Wind walked
free among the columns.
No secret rooms were visible.

My skin reddened, but beyond it
nothing disturbed the darkness.

An ordinary ascent of dust,
dusty shoes.

March, 2001

Campo de Fiori

> A BRUNO
> IL SECOLO DA LVI DIVINATO
> QVI DOVE IL ROGO ARSE

On an early September afternoon
I looked through the window at Campo de Fiori:
the heat of the market was burning out, flowers tired of smiling,
dark stains spread under the tender skins of fruits,
a warm wind carried thin plastic shreds
like ashes, in the middle of the square raised from the ground
stood a blackened bronze man in a long cloak
and hood. It was Giordano Bruno, in his eyes
congealed campfire flames darkened to copper,
having devoured him here precisely four centuries ago
in the name of true knowledge.

Which, as is proved by the facts we observe,
is carried by memory to be reborn in the soul's matrix
and shyly shows itself to God's reflection in its own depths,
and comprehension gushes forth knocking down reason's walls
like a river of flame that flows in both directions.
And the movement stops, the soul clenches
like an impregnated womb, and... We thank the Lord
that we are not so blind, we do not affirm or judge
so therefore know the fire of our hearts is hotter
than all the flames of this world. Silent fields of flowers
ripple beneath our feet, pistils wait for pollen,
their awareness is small but fragrant and durable,
bees carry them and wind as if ashes. Dried out blackberries,
wilting market flowers, the enticing sighs of death
on the misleading roads of knowledge.

November, 2000

The Magi

Through deep snow, numb with cold, led by undiscovered stars
from container to container carrying in plastic bags
recyclable goods like wombs giving birth to things,
using everything that helps them tear themselves away
from the world, whatever is convertible
into moments of ecstasy. Bodies like overworked mules.
Where are they being driven by their anxiety?
Perhaps they know something more, each night watching the cold
sky above their heads, so they build no homes, do not get settled,
do not earn bread by the sweat of their brows?

Directly beneath the North
Star, in one container
at the edge of town, they found a dead child
in a plastic bag. They gave him no gifts
and did not bury him, not wanting
to have any dealings with the police, they were
people of other customs, from another land.
They let him continue suffering quietly for our sins,
unburied, unmourned, unable to rise.
To suffer right away, without words, miracles, sermons,
because everything is already said, everyone is taught,
only action remains. The face of young
Janus in the plastic bag.

Perhaps they know something more?
Perhaps they wait for something to happen?

03/01/2002

Passover

My mother told me how, on the second day of Easter,
she once took me to school with her
because she had no one to leave me with, and I walked
lagging behind her looking carefully at everything. Our street

was almost empty, but when she turned around she saw
an Easter egg in each of my hands, the government forbade
dyeing them then, Stalin had not yet croaked,
as my father used to say. She was afraid: perhaps someone

had deliberately pressed them insidiously into my hands
and some anonymous complaint would shortly reach the Party,
or perhaps someone wanted to show the schoolmaster,
through her son, that Easter was still alive in the catacombs of hearts.

Or perhaps—I think—it was some masculine god, having
passed here at night who took the unsacrificed firstborns
from among those whose doorposts were not marked by blood,
so tired of killing and satiated, that instead of

scratching a knife across my throat (I was after all
a firstborn, though outside, beyond the door, and there
was no blood on my forehead or hands, only baptismal water)
had deigned to leave reflections of his own eggs in my hands.

And because it was a god, those reflections were tangible,
and because of that, the community who worshipped that god
could confidently use his annual passage
for political reasons, to fight led by him.

Of course, that is the classic ideology of terrorism
which is used throughout the world, not only in Egypt or Palestine,
to employ noble goals to justify the means.
I can't say now that those Easter eggs freed me

from slavery, because when I joined the Young Communists
during the day I wasn't noticed but at night I zealously
tore up the flags they had forgotten to lower after their holidays,
slipping through the town with a gang of others like me.

They were fluttered in me by the same wind of hatred.
It was slavery just the same, of course, but there came a time
when I started to understand everything and weigh it.
And converting from a faith in bloody gods

to peaceful nonbelief, I celebrate Easter morning.
Though I haven't gotten used to dyeing eggs, only smashing them.

20/04/2003

Nobody

Not all of my actions are ethical,
befitting a cultured man.

Poking someone's eye out with a stick doesn't suit
someone who wears a pocket square in his jacket
and a rose in his lapel.

Clinging to a sheep's belly while moving through a narrow opening
doesn't suit the man wearing a tuxedo,
Western culture's adept,
who likes good wine and cheese.

But nonetheless that's what happened. And it weighs the conscience?
No. Otherwise we would have been eaten,
we, who so loved ourselves,
until we were lost, took a step back,
retreated, so that our eyes could take in
a greater expanse.

And what we saw was brutality and lies
against gentleness and truth,
the troubadours' chansons (I'd like
to talk about poetry) against "nevertheless it turns."

That was, it appears, the more conscientious view,
that, apparently receding, stepping back
from the self, toward complexity. And toward hedonism?
Toward the audience of the play in which
we ourselves acted? Toward conflicts suited to dramas?

After that is it appropriate for a cultured man
to exterminate politically, measure for measure,
all those who encroached on private property?
Living once, others living just once?
Dizzyingly taking a step forward to the self,

in frenzy biting the shield,
loving one's neighbor not a stranger
in holy ecstasy?

I don't always behave ethically.
My name is Nobody too.

August, 2003

Another Rendezvous

She sat in the armchair as if on a throne, a woman
of unique style: piercing, somewhat tired, eyes,
a radiant face under the net of time's veil
above a long neck, breasts uncovered, sudden
and graceful movements of hands
in delicately crocheted gloves arranging things
in the deepening twilight.
And I (it's not a dream) trying to wake her,
having stopped by (she says—for a while) on my way to autumn.

Not a dream. Then what? I don't know. But I can stop
her hand half way between the glass and shadows
that enter into the arena of our undying love
which she intended to disperse with a ruler's hand...

Now I am their enemy, they try to lift me
from the ground, rocking away desires in their thawing wave—
the flame trembles, October's dusk pours through the window—
she wades against the current which has long been carrying me.
But they don't matter to me, the shadows, I care only about her
who, turning reality into a theatrical scene, strives
to encrust in it a role
which like a cliff will dissect life's turbid water.
That's why, crashed to the ground, I try
to lift her into air vibrating with words,
into things and the will to move them to dissolving twilight,
into the impoverished, arrogant, all-comfortable luxury of doubt,
so that I would force her to forget in my arms,
so that I would move
the years, our meetings separated and filled with foreign feelings,
our own longing, congealing into sadness in our souls.
But my feet press hopelessly into the fog of ideas
while her prop-like armchair looms so firmly on the cliff

that we pass each other again, and I have to give up,
laugh it away, hide the wrong I've suffered under a smile,

hearing how time pours out (or only this meeting's?)
as the beat of our pulses muffles in the submerging night.

November, 2003

Birdie

She rolled out of the egg that was laid
by Leda, afterwards. Black-haired, long-necked, her first
awkward movements already evidenced her coming
grace, penetrating bird eyes and lips, gently
ripening in sweetness for all who would come.

She married a lout who couldn't
satisfy his wife, that's why he scuffled later
with her lover (some say there were more than one) for nine
years "over a woman" or his offended splendor. Because of them
one member of the gang grew famous for his wanderings,
the bedding of elegant women and fidelity to his wife,
one singer went blind, later recovered his sight.
She had to lay on herself (returning through old
people's voices, the Achivi's voluptuous dreams),
adopt part of a man's role (she herself
played only women with her sudden gestures),
as imagined at that time, when in tragedies
men acted the roles of women, of course,
in her life they strived to play men,
much greater than themselves. Some succeeded,
others did not. Because the goddess
had given special privileges
only to Paris. The years passed, and her heroes
changed and aged as she fought with time.

Later, a shepherd she played with in childhood
would sometimes call her Birdie.

July, 2002

Palimpsests

Walking on charcoal footprints following elegant guides
(were souls burned here or something else?) I imagined the world,
later shaved their letters from my cheeks like my beard each morning,
having lathered them with the foam of my vanity.
But the letters burned in my memory as if on a wall,
dragging my pen. Filled
with thoughts not my own, perceptions, imaginings,
burdened with the past and sensations, I weave
my text, watching dejectedly
how letters change their shapes before my eyes,
how meanings merge and separate gulping
the rubbed off, shaved and washed tangle
and how apprehending consciousness adjusts to it...

And you, whose eyes shine with desire white as a snowy field,
are you also a palimpsest? Does my pen, obsessed
with aroused fluid, write into memory a new, original text,
or does it just scrape between the lines, fill lacunae and margins,
and with its foolish zeal arouse
experience like a thick tangle of roots
under the eyes' snowy field?

July, 2001

A Cry in Sleep

No matter what they might say or how it might appear
interesting and reasonable, a dream and that which
you are anxious to call a dream differ greatly.
You can't entangle them so easily. When you cry out
at the top of your voice in a dream, only a muffled moan
will slip out into the stuffy room. Our efforts,
my love, to try to push ourselves beyond this boundary
and there search for explanations of our feelings
are not particularly successful: everything on this side
can be named: texts don't open the curtains,
and especially don't tell even us ourselves
why we do what we do, what we would do with our findings,
and finally, what we are searching for (you asked more than once).
Our essence, not yet overgrown with experiences? Experiences
that could be recreated, imprisoned in stringent forms
and cut out, shaved from memory, from reality?

Our hungers are from there but our actions are from this side.
Dreams giddily rock the drunken will.
What would we write on the erased board — Vita Nuova?
What would we do with our essence — children?

A cry in sleep slips past its boundary greatly weakened.
Experiences collapse into the dream having nowhere else.

October, 2002

Spring in the Middle of Fall

My thoughts grow heavy, curl back into the ground
Bursting before like blossoms and ripening fruits.
Suddenly on the windowsill a tiny bird,
not having managed to fly off to oblivion,
ticks with its claws on the tin parchment
and the soul grows confused.

And the soul blossoms in the fall, but not like
late dahlias, gladioli or asters,
and not like chrysanthemums
but like an insane plum-tree. I shave letters,
write new, unexpected symbols.

Mansion residents look over my shoulder with derision:
there is little here to be believed. But the front
of spring is wide as it is in April, ice fortresses collapse,
the marble of statues chaps and crumbles,
from ever closer gallops bad news.

Mansion residents soberly drink whiskey.
Spring—they say—in the middle of fall?
Interesting, yes, yes, on the way to winter.

November, 2003

A Personal Carnival

> I rhyme
> To see myself, to set the darkness echoing
> Seamus Heaney

It's now carnival season, though like many
I am always knit together with my mask.
I am this or that, or not this, not that.
Sometimes I try too diligently to glance under it,
Sometimes I'm used to it—and how otherwise after all?
And never much feel my part here anyway.
Because when I try to imagine myself without a mask,
I immediately remember our friend Ted
Who, looking into a pond, lacked the literary
Facts to recognize the two-legged thing he saw.
Everything, it seems, would suffice—Narcissus, water,
The reflection in it—not one, not two.
And no associations or preconditions to utter—
Beautiful, ugly, or otherwise judged.
That's why you're anxious to give it a name
And leave it with no references.
If some believe that I'm pretending
Let them look into the mirror in absolute
Darkness without putting on a mask.
You say—he'll know it's him, it's not worth bothering?
He will, if not feeling, how the face streams through time,
Want once to talk to darkness with echoes.

January, 2002

About Beautiful Women

I have a master's degree in sociology and can testify
that all this publicly declared preference for slim women
is distorted, amoral, and statistically false,
that it violates the rights of a large social constituency.
It's all marketing, propaganda, the porno trade...
I can watch that totally bored, nodding my head,
but my blood can be stirred
only by Rubenesque beauties, radiant
with the noblest characteristics of fertility,
affirming a love that does not end in sport,
beauty and goodness contained in their capacious bodies,
kalokagathian, lovingly and indolently moral,
announcing themselves to our unseducable souls
not through the media but in dreams.

May, 2002

The Mermaid's Complaint

When the rain starts I read their verse and weep.
Pale pearls of tears, falling from my eyes,
Roll down my cheeks and drop into the open neck of my tight robe.
I have blossomed like a rose, but the blind world does not see.
Last night he crawled home drunk and today may not come home at all,
And last time his mouth smelled of cheap perfume.
He says his tooth hurts, the one torn out last week…
That's the way girls who hold to no morals scent themselves.
He just called, invited me to go with him to the shore.
I agreed, because the city's heavy air won't let me sleep.
Though things won't end there with such breathing, I feel,
He'll sway and heave sweating until the roosters crow.
How many terrible temptations and dangers lurk in loneliness!
I used to like poetry but now use only prose.
I long only to see beauty but just as I close my eyes
Before me stands that which my sensitive soul condemns—
Under the skin rigid muscles move like the billowing sea,
In my dreams his hairy arms and legs crush me.
Didn't those bards—I think to myself—write too much about love,
If passion rules us and power does not ask for consent.
Life itself is to blame for that, but poets are also guilty:
They seduce souls, then cast them out into the dirt.
It is raining so sadly outside, but those images do not calm.
Ah, the tub is full, time to return to my own element.

September, 2003

The Fruit of Concord

Then, perhaps in spring, the gardens blooming, their fruits
ripening in imaginations and chafing with stiff rinds,
with eyes herding soft clouds that evoke things,
they drew near. I held my soul in my hand,
shaped like a heavenly fruit,
the hologram of the apple reflecting in their eyes,
and extended it to her who was both blossom and fruit.
And she accepted my gift, and let me glorify
her divinity, having burned in my heart images filled
with wonder and pushing myself through people,
and I venerated her, filling my words
with all the feelings I had. The rivals
smiled bewitchingly. And she set me
free and gave me the woman I longed for.

And there were no wars, because it was only my soul,
one among many, not especially significant,
but filled with fascination and empty of features.

November, 2000

Fifty-Year-Old Women

You have to wait a long time to know them,
lurk in the thickets of experience, senses tensed,
clenching the heart's fading heat in your chest.
Their souls are cautious and fearful as ermine,
breakable, even though they have shells,
in their hearts more indulgent benevolence
than fire, which could be extinguished
by an accidental wind, and in their movements
less passion than skill. They are the first to see
the one who lies in wait. On their lips the simplest words
ring more luxuriously than these lines.
They spend more on cosmetics
and keep longer company with mirrors.
They press close so gently, so cautiously,
boldly and timidly, as if hoping for something
and expecting nothing, that the soul stirs.
You have to wait a long time to know them,
but there are no more elegant creatures in the world.

November, 2000

Clinical Observations

There are things not suited to poetry.
Even if you talked about death,
a theme especially favored in youth,
or doublings, schizophrenia in other words.
Only adapted scenes force their way into poetry,
tailored to the author's psyche. Everything else
remains behind a blind wall of white gowns.
Everything else is not suited to poetry.

Or remains on opposite sides of the wall, when the soul
splits in two, one still tries to respond to you,
the other is already in the beyond, purgatory, always
moans and weeps in the living body. They don't meet.
When asked, why do you moan, it answers
surprised: me? I'm moaning? forgive me,
I won't any more. And again neglects the body
for that of purgatory. Such an "I" is not suited to poetry.
It can't be found in Dante's taxonomy.

Or two stanzas of some old poem about
loneliness and death remain, which
also are not suited to poetry.

December, 2001

Petaludes *

An indolent brook down the slope, small ponds, waterfalls.
But nymphs do not bathe here, even though just now,
it appears, they hid, disappeared in the thicket,
like thousands of the goddess's moths
hidden in the hollows, under leaves, in rock clefts
(their backs spruces, and underwings, red).
And hundreds of the wingless, with flashes and applause
raising their sisters into the air
above Phoebe's island, growing out of the water
(God's fiery seed fused its gravel and shells),
mottled hordes scuttling back and forth, rummaging,
the backs and underwings of each one unique.

Our souls will fly away, I say,
and will be blinded also
by the light on the other side, and will scatter like nymphs,
unable to find their world, like petaludes,
not knowing where to alight, where to fold their wings.

December, 2000

* *"Petaludes," in Greek the word for butterflies, is a shaded valley on the Isle of Rhodes, where many butterflies of night live.*

Aegean Wine

On cobblestones, asphalt paths,
then down beach gravel to the first pier,
and on it deeper into the sea.
It grew dark, drizzled, memories
began to unravel from the darkness of memory.
Maybe it's time to turn back?

We fended off hated order with inspired chaos,
dizzy with wine and our hard truths.
Now we look around with wonder, listen, touch shapes
which, it seems, are tendered for our thoughts, our speech.
They were young,
dizzy with passion and victory,
forgot to change the sails.
Here is the Baltic Sea, people living near it
speak different languages but share customs.
At the symposiums, Mediterranean wine,
wine from the Aegean. He jumps into the water
from the promontory cliff. And we must begin
our sober everyday routines.

September 2001

Pyromaniacs

Virgin forests burn in the depths of their old souls,
cities and ravaged villages that did not hold back their siege,
they burn slowly, with a persistent flame, not finding what is real,
with which they could suddenly stand before their eyes. And here—

the most ordinary flame, ignis vulgaris, blazes
like a torrent of poetry, breaking through barriers,
like a play seen from a palace balcony by someone
looking at a city gone to ghosts long ago, and two

fires braid together like a caduceus, the catharsis
meanders down the hillside like a river of lava
toward an old soul, which flinches
and slowly comes to realize, but too late.

April, 2002

Honor and Justice

Honor is for the wanderer. It weighs
nothing. It is like a butterfly with razor wings
on one's shoulder. It does not increase the burden
even changing his person to stone, weighing his thoughts
down with certitudes. It is always there,
in the threads of nerves, images of relationships.
It is sometimes more important than life.

Justice is for the sedentary. It protects
his wealth and person, sometimes the rather stale
space of his existence, it meets the arrogant wanderer
with sword and scales, weighs according to
codices, papers, and witnesses
in whose eyes honor has long not shone.
Because wealth is heavy as living.
It is sometimes more important than life.

It happens, that the sedentary tries to defend
honor with justice. How regrettable.

June, 2001

Copyright ©

I come closer to him, lying comfortably
on the beach: eyes docile,
legs folded under his powerful trunk,
short golden fur, around his horns
a ruffled mane like a tow of wool
tempting me to sink my fingers in, press
against his fragrant body, feel its power and warmth.
Forgetting myself I caress his neck, with my fingers
touch folds of skin. He lazily lifts his head, looks
into my eyes so tenderly that I can't resist
straddling his broad back, wiry hair
tickling my thighs and crotch, penetrating my lips,
making me squirm and...
Suddenly he jumps up and plunges into the sea, white
froth splashes from his chest to my folded legs,
horror and lust clench my throat...
At last he climbs onto Crete's sun-filled shore,
I slide exhausted onto the soft grass and, oh God!
He kneels above me carefully
on all fours, and I suddenly feel how hot,
thick and slippery his thing is as it penetrates me
tenderly and persistently, copying the ritual
that Gaea has assigned to the living,
and how my joyful womb already reads, apprehends, sorts
his liquid shape...

Daedalus finishes his work, night pants heavily,
muted sighs walk the corridors of the palace: Pasiphaë...
My bosom, as if lifted by them like the sea...
He finishes upholstering the wood with skin, golden fur glistens.
I touch the new mask impatiently, my lust
spurs on the laboring craftsman.
Art is an imitation, a copy of the works of gods.
Minos, with what desires are your saps poisoned?

I crawl through the small door, lay down on soft pillows,
the bull already squirms in the arena. Quod licet? © ?
What shape now, what message
will my greedy womb scan now,
what will it ripen for a small harmonious world?

I wove Europa on the bull's back,
Danaë drinking rain like parched ground,
Leda swooning under the swan,
the way Pallas had taught me,
only spinning my thread more thinly,
stretching my warp more tightly,
moving the bobbin more nimbly.
My succulent pictures of passion surpassed
her boring Areopagus with the dry voices of old men.
My imagination lifted me from the earth
but not toward heaven to the gods, bored on their thrones,
did not fall as low as grandiose self-portraiture.
Everyone saw it.

And she said then: be a spider,
ugly creature with eight limbs in the sea of imagination,
hanging between heaven and earth.
And now my textile—
only a strange pattern of the psyche, a net
for your thoughts, dear reader.

September, 2001

Cave Phenomena

They say carbonic acid melts soft rocks,
they flow away on underground rivers, drip from stalactites,
grow stalagmites, in coves
jam together as small coffins like junks,
seen from an airplane,
and in those small coffins—just lift the lid—
you'll see your days,
the shapes of your thoughts, as if cerements
of somewhat whiter fog, a thin membrane
lying on former illusions.

And in the mouths of rivers!...
How nobly they would float out to sea,
would meet the first wave...

And my loves sleep there with eyes closed,
with smiles barely visible in the corners of their mouths,
reflecting
in shimmering surfaces...

And my verses sleep
in the printer's paint cases...

Time's acids ate away the soft rocks
from the monolith of consciousness—
the caves weave, branch like a labyrinth
in a once firm mass,
melted rocks drip
in tears from your eyes, roll down your cheeks, leaving
funeral membranes and empty spaces
to lay down the world
in the hour of death,
to begin a new life,
arrange decorations and raise
the curtain of the new performance,

or equip offices and begin to expand commerce,
or see the house, the grove,
highway or brook cave in.

And then swing away in rivers toward the mouths
slowly, somewhat ceremoniously or even pompously—
in each coffin a poem or a medal,
or some other small fetish—
thinking: if only we don't tip over
in the first wave.

June, 2009

About Gods and People

I don't know, don't know... They say it's a cudgel, Eros' fiery dart,
ball lightning cleaves the stagnant darkness,
deadened consciousness, chaos, and a new world emerges,
or, they say, they sit in low voices
vibrating the cave's door until it does not hold
and hidden goodness gushes, to, they say, sun-drenched valleys,
and that's every time...

But leaving me they leave emptiness behind,
half-collapsed corridors
in abandoned buildings.
I gave birth to seven children for him (for him?).
He was drunk every day, every other beat me, screaming
across the entire hostel: whore, I'll killlll you,
you ruined my whole life!...
And strayed to other women, while I was still fertile,
then left, went to another city,
now, they say, he routs through garbage cans.

I'm not reborn like everything around me.
My darkness doesn't thicken, rot, sour, grow listless,
doesn't tear up forms, my darkness doesn't recover
its primordial black purity... Empty
never ending caves, Plato would go mad in them,
empty rooms, broken glass, torn wallpaper.
I'm not nature, no goddess, I have my beginning and my end,
not everything rebuilds itself in me, not everything breaks down,
I don't have Semele's pride, silliness, curiosity,
there was enough of his seed, almost by force
with threats to kill me
(how could he imagine himself equal to the gods
if not by killing me?) A dry wind
wanders through the halls, from which hopes,
bewitching images, perceptions have moved...
I don't know, don't know... Just to sing
like a bird calling to another...
Most likely just that.

January, 2010

A Shabby Dwelling

The air is thicker here, fragrances
loom like a former forest of conceptions.

Though I could always find her scent
through the deluding perfumes of ideas
with love's perfect sense of smell.

Always grasping the tightly-stretched reins,
barely across the span away from desired things,
always restrained at the last minute.
She said she liked to walk on the edges of knives,
trying not to collapse into my (oh if only into my!) passion
which had no bottom, no boundaries, no response.

Once in my vision her naked body glittered
like waxed marble. I began to turn...
Not into prey, no, but a tool, just as earlier
I had been transformed into the tool of my desire — with no
Other hungers, thoughts, identities, realities —
animal on the reins.

I felt completely normal then, led down the street
by another woman. I could smell her from a distance,
as always, surrounded by a fence that did not contain her fragrance.
Her graceful quick steps rang in my blood.

After that I don't remember. When we had
almost passed by one another, I jumped onto her
wanting to embrace her with my front legs, and yelping
she staggered under my body's weight, the guide mumbled
that I had never done that before. I was wearing a muzzle.
She didn't recognize me. Our eyes did not meet.
Our eyes did not meet.

ZDANYS

Didn't recognize me? Let her try
to remember. For if I wasn't the only one
like that under the reins... let her try. Circe.

The body is a shabby dwelling
and even desire is more stable.

September, 2004

A Discussion About Lions

She said she saw on television how a lioness
is impregnated: she is first pollinated by one, then by
his brother, and later by a stray. No emotions were involved.
Probably because—as the narrator commented—
lionesses rarely conceive on the first try.

I answered that once Atalanta (fugiens),
nursed on bear's milk, unsurpassable,
promised to marry the one who could outrun her,
and she killed the ones who lost.
Then someone named Melanion or Hippomenes, who had
three golden apples from the Hesperidian gardens, ran
and threw them one by one just when she caught up
and he reached the finish line alive. (I don't know,
perhaps it was gentleness and love, hands
on your desired body.) And they got married
and constantly made passionate love everywhere, and once
they did that in one of Zeus' temples, and the angered
god turned them into lions (Zeus and the Greeks for some reason
believed that only leopards could impregnate lionesses),
that is to say, they would live in chastity.

The apples were stolen, and god, as always,
lacked an understanding of nature. So let them be lions.
It's only a form,
one of many.

April, 2004

The Goddess of Oblivion

It's a woman, hanging laundry
on a rope, flapping in the wind, damp,
for a moment stuck with what is no longer there.

Ugly, angular, unattractive

our mother
of oblivion.

January, 2005

Outlines

1.
I can name everything,
can outline everything.

2.
Even your oval belly I encircle
With the oval of a poem, "my dear."

3.
Language from Culture, which belongs to us,
which we created, carefully tended, whose pinnacle

4.
we darkened with the clouds of secret rituals,
and we forbade them to witness

5.
for those whose creative powers arise on their own from nothing,
whose swollen ovals encompass, even give birth to us...

6.
It is hardest to perceive that. How we are born—
with Culture or without?

7.
If without, then everything is determined by initiations,
which we fulfill in secret and without hardship.

8.
But each of us has experienced
how little they change.
That's why doubt remains.

9.
And what if with? Could Culture
conceal itself in these strange creations?

10.
Then we enclose the mother and child in the oval
and solemnly announce the doctrine of the second birth.

11.
Yes, we tamed nature, fettered your strengths,
with rituals bound the demigods
who laid you—
we know it, don't lie.

12.
We transformed them into wooden idols, and now
with our magical dances don't let them come to life again,

13.
because we know, on full moon nights you still dream of
their long fecund organs and hands that grasp your backs.

14.
That's why we can't calm down,
that's why the worm of suspicion, like self-
deception, gnaws at our brains.

15.
That's why we rape, murder, display power and rule,
until we conceive that this all is natural—
so much death everywhere that it cannot be multiplied.

16.
She has outlined everything in a tight oval
which it is better not to see, because our rituals don't function.

17.
My dear, to protect myself
from choosing your freedom from your governance of me,

18.
from fear, from doubting myself, from your
inclination to surrender to demigods in my imagination,
I surround your image with an oval as if on an old postcard,

19.
I meditate, incense the gods, burn
my heart's desires like the sun burns the desert,

20.
I break the attachments
and stuff myself with tranquility...

21.
But the worm gnaws through it.

22.
I cast off norms, truths, regulations, go out of my mind,
my will, guilts and beliefs, find delight only in semblances,

23.
reel in ecstasies or shudder in catharses
until the worm suddenly stirs and calls me.

24.
Finally, numb with horror, I see
how desire outlines me within you like a womb.

March, 2005,
New Guinea,
The Abelam Forest

About Starlings After Yet Another Five Years

I live now like a starling
in a small computer box,
cast my songs into the world net
far, wide, though fewer ears probably
hear them than yours, my brother,
which you warble on the roof fluttering
your wings home again after winter,
transformed into a beckoning voice.
That's not how it works for me, and even
the changing seasons don't stir my feelings,
as if I had left their circle and had ended up
on a straightaway, at whose end
is the small strip that separates realities...
The way myth pretending to be history
confuses reason and truth,
fractured time turning into a straight line,
and so my poetic identity
tempts the virtual bird
to jug all year (out of habit?)
on a branch gilded by intoxication.

April, 2005

Portrait

The paint cracked
like Leonardo's, Vermeer's
like Rembrandt's.
Time is our disease. Unfulfillments.
And if—I say—some small patch falls off
who will know how to return it to a forgetful past?
Will restorers reconstruct color,
variable semitones?
And if they do, won't time
change them at a different rate?

Passions are our disease. Unsatisfied.
Fissuring the coating,
transforming us into puzzles
in the banality of mirrors...

And if—I say—in that patch is a former
reflection of your soul or the shadow of a lover's face?

Turning back you'd say you saw
how quickly you disappeared into the crowd,
as if you had dissolved in paint.

May, 2006

The Faceless

No, if that's believing I won't confess to it.
I need knowledge, need a guide—
the land of the dead is full of error,
it is thick with souls, likenesses.
I don't remember her face.
But some succubus can pretend to be her,
easily adapt a mask.
You at least had seen her, your Euridice, you knew
how she looked, why you were descending there, arrows
of your songs had a purpose. But I did not.
I suspect that it's my soul's
face, which mirrors don't reflect,
which can be seen only on the surface of Lethe,
on the other shore, emptied of words.
Each succubus is able to pretend
to be her, the way women do here, in illusion,
without a sense of foreboding,
intently watching my movements, my lies.
They hate the faceless but want to be her.
And I for a moment want to be deceived,
become acquainted, almost trust...
It's not enough for me to know she's in the land
of the dead, if I believed in you, or elsewhere.
I'd want to see her, rest calmly in her arms,
even if for eternity.
My aimless songs are about that.

I'm not speaking to explain anything here.

January, 2007

Autumn's Flowers

Dahlias, gladioli and asters,
blossoms lifted with dignity to the cooling air,
and your multicolored cap,
with all their hues
radiant above the garden.
You say: this autumn
stole my hair
and scattered it in spiderwebs
on stalks of dry grass,
on passionate memories,
on brightening waters.
Men are finishing picking
the small garden's harvest,
the barrow squeaks with cranes.
—It's hardest to endure uncertainty—
you say with dignity to air filled with sunshine.
A cold wind blows through
the dahlias, gladioli, and asters.

November, 2007

A Cookie for Persephone

for Vaiva, in memoriam

I looked at the small green light on the empty screen,
outside the window hung a somber webbed December mist,
the radio talked about how to bake ginger cookies.
Clunk — the cellphone's trap slammed suddenly: "She's gone."
Little mouse, little mouse
take the ginger cookie,
carry it through the deepest caves,
lay it at the feet of Hades,
at Persephone's.
Say: the soul of she who comes now
is whiter than snow,
hands with palms offered up,
the heart clutching nothing.
Say: just do not ask her
to open her eyes,
let the world remain as it is
beyond those gates of bone.
Wandering through blossoming meadows
after you, Persephone,
they saw such harmony,
were flooded with such beauty,
that the underworld kingdom
would be filled with light
and suddenly you'll think
that it is time to return.

14/12/2008

The Square

> *Desolate is the roof where the cat sat...*
> Ezra Pound, Canto XXXIX

An empty square, where the monument stood,
there's no pedestal, pissed on by dogs,
wind brings a scrap of thin plastic,
it unexpectedly jumps into the monument's place
and once again settles down beyond it. The subconscious
sucks up reality—I tell my young companion
now no one will be able to explain
what, how, and why it changed.
What, how, and why it lives
in someone's memory—as time passes,
it looks more and more like a graveyard,
the earth devouring tombstones.

January, 2008

Vita Nuova

Morning's hinges creak, waking me,
Titans moor on the ocean's bottom,
and Phoebus rolls out of the cave of ideas
in a glittering chariot
as if in a new Ferrari through the factory gates
into a fresh world revised by the morning papers...

And the oblivions of the abyss swallow night's dreams
together with those who lifted their heads
before our gods, paying no attention
to financial markets, economic indexes,
commodity prices, currency exchange rates.
The battle is won—Gaia's sons
are cast by the gods to Tartarus.
A new life explodes in images.

Phoebus' steeds never dreamed of such speed.

January, 2008

A Troubled Year

That year the heavens sent many omens
promising disastrous events,
which our decaying morality demanded,
but the year ended
according to all the calendars
and nothing happened.

Except that the supreme interpreter
of omens died.

April, 2008

Also Died

> to Gerardo, for reasons of literary scholarship

The water in the pond died of longing
having waited in vain for an intent gaze.

Love died in that water
as bodies entwined.

The poet died on the shore
having stopped admiring himself.

The light in the eyes died, the deep of the pupils
gone opaque, having found no reflection.

Billions of gray cells dying carried our words
to the other side of the mirror's glass.

The hard disk was broken
by the virus of self perception.

June, 2006

Wanting to Be

    you must be like everyone else—
at least a catholic
at least a moral christian (depends on the place)
at least a jew
at least a muslim
at least a prometheus
you must love your neighbor as yourself
and yourself—endlessly (like a christian)
and unlove a stranger
if resources are not sufficient
you must say: and how will I now and how will I now
and how will I now die and where will I go? and then
you will have to answer immediately: I
will rise from the grave with a body spackled with impurities
and will be brought to the last judgment—
if you want to be like everyone else don't try
to avoid juridical procedures
(though they too depend on the place)—
so will be brought to trial flipping the finger in his pocket;
ha, I got my body back so screw you
at least (for) a circus man (these stunts)
at least (for) a social activist (others?)
at least (for) a native (kalashnikovs and whiskey)
at least (for) a roundworm in its place (good feeding)
    you must love yourself passionately and gently
at least a representative of an opposing fratria
at least as I said a prometheus
    (a wife for one people's gratitude for the other)
    you must love yourself—l o v e
    and if I have already rebelled against god
    or the gods then with full stature like the titans
    with full stature which is not at all low
at least (for) a child of nature (a prize)
at least (hangovers for) a club hopper
at least (for) a frequent lover (a discount coupon)

at least (coffee) a buyer of the morning paper
    and its reader (pridefully)
at least a television watcher (chopped off heads)
at least a radio listener (speaking)
at least (laurels for) an award-winning poet
at least him who seeks a career (the grace of heaven)
    and struggles with the angel on the stairs
    or otherwise reads the bible (amen)
at least one who goes to church on Sundays
at least a buddhist (zen) or krishna (hare)
at least (steering wheel) one who can't manage without a car
at least one who doesn't believe in god (catechismvsa)
    and similar foolishness (prasty szadei)
    we require loving oneself
    does that require resourcefulness? no
    but we need it to suggest to others
    the successes we've had, being loved
    or at least deserving of envy, or else
    respected out of fear (just in case)
at least achilles to the heel
at least a heel to teeth (to another)
at least to Nobody
    you must l o v e yourself.
    wanting to be

                                              June, 2008

---

* *Catechismvsa Prasti Szadei (Simple Words of the Catechism)* by Martynas Mažvydas *(The Old Lithuanian Catechism, 1547)* is the first book published in the Lithuanian language.

Speleologists

We bought ropes then,
waterproof lanterns,
took along a few additional essential things
(not books, since they'd ask there: which
would you take to a deserted island
or to some moon? No,
we didn't take any)
and descended into the underground.
Black water, blind fish, short echoes.
No naiads in the grotto's shade. No
ideas on the walls. Perhaps they all remained
in the books we didn't take? That we forgot.
We felt betrayed,
each of us saw a great deal
but the images, it seems, all different.
That's why we couldn't agree,
create knowledge, lay down
the fundamentals of speleology.
Or was it because we were amateurs
without predetermined assumptions
that would explain what surrounded us?
Only darkness surrounded us,
carved by tufts of lantern light.
Later we fell asleep on a raft
from some sort of fumes
and the river somehow carried us to the surface.

June, 2008

I Met that Starling Later in Dublin

He tiptoed warbling in the November
airport, just past the arrivals door,
on occasion trundling to escape
approaching shoes, sometimes
turning his beak towards something,
but holding it back at the last minute,
understanding the target wasn't something to eat.

I have nothing to add about myself.
I had wandered in there for just a moment.

November, 2008

Confrontation in the Museum

Dickheaded Cypress,
(I am addressing the god hiding in us,
controlling our hands and minds,
or perhaps them both—Apollo and Dionysus), how long
is the way from your coarse amulet,
with the body crucified by two genders
conjuring a blunt world,
to this marble maiden with firm breasts
and youth's back, Hellene,
reviving the body in the fire of our glance
betraying the master who strode long ago
on the golden rooftop in moonlight and still
how long the time to our
barbaric conceptualizing,
in single-use forms suppressing
unnecessary small ideas
like private sexual organs
controlling our hands and minds.

April, 2009

The Transfigured Stairs

There were only three stairs to the porch
but they suddenly began to shine differently,
as if in a new light that holds things,
torn from memory in old photographs,
and the house remained in another time,
became unreachable,
and my "I" cracked, liquified.
Lord, you won't be able to put a foot on it,
won't walk across the image fixer's lake, won't step
into the soul's home on the other side
whose window shutters
are banged so hard by the heavens' winds.

June, 2009

The Followed

Turning around I saw my footprints—
One foot a man's, the other a bird's.
No, no, this has nothing to do
with those romantic ravings
that are supposedly used to stuff poetry.
Both of my feet are normal: the left, the right.
Then I'm being followed. Who is it?
I began to study ornithology.
It turns out the footprint is a falcon's (remaining
alongside my foot in the sand,
the stretch of sidewalk, asphalt, my pillow,
near the small rug by the door, near my bed,
on the remains of my memory, on that which was).
Horus, is it you who chase
the poor rabbit through the desert of shallowing sand
one foot a man's, the other a bird's?

Gods never answer.
You do that for them.

June, 2006

Family History

In a spacious basement, to which
lead narrow stairs,
behind opaque windows, a long table
at which the whole family would fit:
children, grandchildren, great-grandchildren,
and a massive hearth so all
would be warm and cozy together
in the burrow underground, away from eyes.
They did not sit
at that table, didn't light the hearth,
scattered, spread out, having
nothing to say to each other. And he,
who had created the space to unite them,
is now in the cramped basement, which
you will not reach on any stairs,
only through the earth,
that restores us to life with no
memory, no soul.

October, 2009

The Arrival Hall

Suddenly a light-haired child sees me
and starts to run with arms raised: "grandpa!"

Just like his father ran. Just like I
will soon run into your
smothering embrace, death.

May, 2007

Don't Talk Loudly

She says—talk as if you're talking to yourself...

We walk through the halls of the museumed mansion to the garden,
then through the gates into the meadows,
a small bird or two lifts from beneath our feet
like an inadvertent uttered word.

Suddenly she calls out: I felt jealous
when you admired that woman's face in the cameo...
But it's your face there—I say—
you travel through the ages in the cradle of my heart
on the other side of forms,
on the other side of the heart,
on the other side of my...

Don't talk loudly—she whispers—I'll hear...

December, 2008

The Christmas Bird

So colorful, with a pin in place of a foot,
with a tail of glittering glass filaments,
each year flew from the unreachable cupboard
and perched on the Christmas tree,
and sang to me about a different, more beautiful life.
And that's how over several years it weaved its nest
in the thickets in my head...
And I got used to waiting for it, learned to miss it, to connect
it to things ever dearer to my heart.
It was the first cavity, the first nesting box
in the monolith of my consciousness,
a warehouse of dreams, a depot of desires,
a catalog of images,
the first emptiness.

As if I remember its voice...

December, 2009

Haiku, Senryu, and Other Very Short Poems

The current—
"day and night, summer and winter"
complains the river fish.

And out of the past
wind carries blossom petals
that blanket the stream.

Blossoms drift away
on the river. This nonsense
is ending once more!

I say: you're lovely.
The nightingale after all
does not follow notes.

Far from the earth
but not closer to heaven.
Valleys drown in blossoms.

Petals of tulips.
Angels—merely emptiness
of our consciousness.

The blackbird's song placed
a period on the text
of insomnia.

❋

The furies' bright eyes
found both of us in the dark
of the far mountains.

❋

Beneath copper skies
on a muggy summer night...
Everything passes.

❋

The sparrow chases
a fly for her nested brood,
in the church—High Mass.

❋

The loud lawnmower
cuts off the heads of daisies,
gathers them in bows.

❋

The cat has been pitched
to the pond after a frog
by her own instinct.

❋

The rains of summer.
Both of us home with the cat,
a snail at home too.

❋

It is still July
but grasshoppers already
chirping sing the end.

A white butterfly
against the fence staves—
a violin melody.

A white butterfly
against the fence staves—
a petal in the wind.

The storm's far away,
yet my mind's devastated
by a soundless squall.

The stairs of temples
are much steeper in August.
Carp at the surface.

And for twenty yen
you can enter into
the Buddha's belly.

Cicadas droning.
Me with The Lonely Planet
in my backpack.

The passing freight train
rattles on the truck's windows
the dry season's rain.

Small fish
in Lake Ohrid,
great poets
on the bridge in Struga.

Your book has many
things, but the dividing mark
here is simply you.

Down along your cheek
red as a maple I roll
in an angry tear.

From the foam of dream
emerging into semblance
we smile so shyly.

The river carries our
two faces under the bridge.
One more October.

Cicadas chirp.
The telephone doesn't work.
Edo.

Fields of rice.
In one of them sprouted
beds of gravestones.

The sun's small rabbit
hops along the back of chairs
into the autumn.

The flood of words has
ended. Autumn's full moon is
void as an echo.

With fingernails of
leaves I hold fast to the tree
outside the window.

Who has so thickly
filled up the pine forest and my
memory with smoke?

flow of wind
flow of senses
flood of yellow

Mounted orchestra—
sounds shuffling along the ground
together with shit.

Gray rain
on a leaden sea.
I return to you.

She stands at the top
of the stairs, young, short-skirted.
My mother lies dead.

Plant trees in Edo
and the cicadas will chirp
when their time comes.

They migrate in zeroes
and ones in autumn
like my poetry.

Look, how your own shell
empties because of all my
desires.

The world is empty.
So I fill you again with
meaning, mountain ash.

Lithuanian fish
fingering syllables
in an autumn lake.

Sparrows scatter
like tiny beads
in Rosario.

The world that flourished
and shrank just recently is
expanding again.

Water carries time
with the dust from a soiled rag
away down the sink.

The dog of the house
reads the smells of the forest
in instinct's volume.

Warm January.
The ground is soft and slimy.
I don't want to die.

Bottle of whiskey,
I'm empty already too
but not yet lucid.

Lakes beneath the ice,
it's time to chop holes in it—
all the world is one.

In winter's sick room
the finch is finishing to
recover from it.

The knife of morning
slices through the powdered crust,
the sun slips away.

The wood is piled up,
the road for the Sun to climb
to the skies is paved.

>					2003–2010

IV

fetters of ice
creaking gravely elevate
a new world

A Partial Eclipse

The sun's light thins,
the sky pales, solitary clouds gray,
the air wisps among the trees, more space appears,
birds hush,
darkness' jaws mouth the golden disk,
night's luminary blackens, prepares to cast a shadow
on smoky glass,
beyond which my soul, equally partially darkened,
hopes that the jaws grasping it will soon pull back,
but no. This covering body leaves
its heavy shadow, year after year having
absorbed accumulated sorrows,
and only when I pull away
will it pull away too.

20/03/2015, 12:30

Golem's Crew

Beyond the bars a terrifying freedom,
limiting circumscriptions, and on this side
of the rib cage, of the casing with an agitating
layer of fat, some ruler's
portrait on the façade (plump lips,
a sagging double chin, bags under his eyes)
we, prisoners of our formless bodies,
conscripts of another world: an aging
senator, an honest peasant, a crooked innkeeper,
and some more difficult to recognize; in all, let's say,
seven of them or of sensations,
giving birth to desire and constant confusion,
galley slaves chained to move
this giant body's joints...

In the hall alongside the bars of ribs (dark
hallways lead into it — the mind's eye cannot
see those who wander them), handles, levers, movers,
masks hung on the walls,
with one of which covering your formless face
you stand before your own consciousness.
You don't know how you choose them, don't notice how
and when you change them: everything happens on its own:
environment, school, culture, reality, habits...
A name. Golem flinches and wakes,
his mouth opens slowly,
chews something for a long time and swallows,
at long last says: "I".

May, 2015

The Passion According to Pilate

so are you saying that he's your son just as he says he's yours
are you a god or demon I don't know I don't care
I don't speculate about the future I have to maintain order
I'm not avenging today just punishing but this case is unique
the wall of life and death separates us he says he's like your
son and still living and only saying it connects him to you
who recently roamed at night killing infants
so you deserve to be punished though there's no other way
to get hold of you only through the one who speaks and begs
to be punished for something he hasn't done
he says he's going to die so the sins of the whole world
would be forgiven so I understand yours as well the revenge
an eye for an eye a tooth for a tooth which you like would be if they
crucified him though I am concerned only with punishing
those who kill at night and hope for benefits for themselves during
the day no one will avoid trial though it appears you wanted
once again to muddle footprints and play out retribution
preparing a bloody feast for the one who is born who is saying
no you won't fool me though some gods and people
accepted this sacrifice of blood and saw it as reward
it's just one more act of terrorism even if carried out
by a local king then for him who is saying I wash
the blood from my hands he chose this road himself
I feel for him and am sorry now he's probably not guilty
I just don't know if I'll be able to wash away my memory
because I too in my heart wanted the same thing he wanted
just doubted that this was the only road because to believe
in sayings is not allowed by my current duties and procedures
so let's get this finished quickly get the old accounts settled
I can't stamp around for long here having crossed jurisdictions
so it's not revenge not trial not reward but redemption
let's seal the old world with the blood of this innocent so armed
gods don't return to it again so no one would never and for no
reason again speak in their names not kill for them
let's finish up quickly and forget and forget and forget

04/04/2010

Exodus

Reading poems, slinging wisecracks
into the night sky, autographs, dinner,
a spot of wine, pleasant conversations...
Later we go out into the blind darkness, search
with our feet for the gravel of the path, some sort of owl
chopping the air with her trenchant squalls... Ah,
there's some sort of bush here!... perhaps charred over
because it's so mingled with the night?... someone's shoulders!...
(is it you?) and someone else's arm...
As if I had heard the voice
of a person who isn't here,
who cannot be here, then another's
and still another's... "Where are we all going? Let's
hurry home, leave the dark to the owls,"—
someone I can't see says. My hand
grabs the veranda's railings.
Though "It's not that veranda," that same
voice says, one I'd heard before,
unfamiliar, never forgotten, "but we nonetheless
welcome you warmly inside."

July, 2015

February 28th

The month would end today
bringing winter and everything else down
if it were not a leap year, a cogwheel
with an additional tooth, tomorrow
another February day will dawn...
What will you do during it? It will be Monday.
I'll finish my daily chores, will repeat rituals—
some offensive and some pleasant routines,
an ordinary day, appended, gifted,
but not suggesting different behavior—to starve
the body by fasting, meditate or pray,
give in to orgies, gorge,
get drunk until you scratch the earth,
confess to readers
you've lied every other day of the year...
Ordinary calendas,
customs indicate nothing as well.
So what, will we let it pass unrecognized,
tepid and meaningless, as we have until now
for all our lives?!

Today is still only the twenty-eighth,
let's wait, tomorrow will be more reasonable
and the day after we will have forgotten it.

28/02/2016

Spring Readings

Spring raged, apple trees blossomed.
The scene outside the window reflected itself
in the glass of the bookcase doors
together with me, together with
the names of those dear to me
on the spines and their faces,
no longer on this side of life;
pens between their fingers stiff
from writing meandered
as if drunk until they staggered
past the boundaries of places only they knew:
one did not return from the sea at dawn,
another declared his wisdom to a customs agent
and disappeared with him down a tunnel's maw,
another melting into mist above a swamp,
creating from words
such a familiar but parallel world...
The view from the window was enough for me,
the white raging of spring
at a safe distance, beyond the glass,
but I would have liked to ask
what signs, what meanings
(where) the boundaries' materials were left?
What kind of place (white as spring?)
is this earth of misunderstanding?

April, 2015

On Both Sides

I saw her and know she saw me
through the glass of the bar window that separated us:
one of us sat inside eyes stuck to the screen,
the other stood in the street as a November rain fell.
Fingers moved like a spider on the keyboard as if
searching the world wide web for a body to touch
with its hairy tentacles. Suddenly "that other"
popped up there, on the screen, waved
joyfully, as if reaching some goal.
You'll ask: did they redouble? No, it was the same
scene, but only as if in different mirrors,
a slightly different angle, but what's the difference—
the image won't reach you, won't borrow
your hands, because none of us can cross the boundary
or at least throw a stone at the glass. It's more
possible with language, if the image is possible,
but do life juices flow in those paintings,
which would nourish the roots of words and straighten
stems, lift delicate leaves, thicken the syntax,
do they pulsate somehow between those zeros and ones
(Battery low—a window pops up—OK.), does
it tempt the zeroes to open, and the ones to penetrate deeper,
to pour into an unprogrammable rage? Yes—it responds—it's pulsating:
"Battery low." The screen suddenly goes out
Blowing us from the bar stool and the sidewalk
back into the cold November dusks.

November, 2015

One Spring

Spring arouses hope and tempts us to walk
along paths of grass stems and tree buds.
The abbey's garden rises
as if to a new life.
The earth drinks in thoughts about death like water.
Novitiates talk about something and laugh.
The basilica looks different, the coriander
it seems changed colors.
The world is different, stranger.
If I were a physicist, I could tell
if the composition of sunlight had changed,
if the air remained the same,
not including pollution which, of course, always grows.
Perception has changed.
I'd be more naïve, would ask the novitiates
how they understand that same Book,
but I know I wouldn't understand their answer
just as they don't understand my question.
Perhaps a conversation about garden plants
would be more understandable? I wonder.
When perception changed, things would hardly
maintain around themselves an aura of constancy,
even the simplest—a pencil or scissors...
Knowing has changed.
There are other things in my thoughts,
other experiences lifted
even through a similar labyrinth of warehouses,
led by different emotions...
Values have changed which
for me and for them strange worlds are lacking,
though none of us is satisfied with that one.
Spring arouses hope,
various hopes like every year to walk
along paths of grass stems and tree buds,
but reality absorbs them
like wine turned into water.

March, 2016

Milk

When they poured us into small bags,
from the One we became units,
from tons we became liters,
as if we had returned to udders.
From cows we became small bags
with colored labels
and bar line codes
betraying our price.

Yesterday two young men of Asian appearance
rang at my door and asked if I was a priest,
I said that no, the priest lives on the first floor,
then one of them still pulled out a
"Short Dictionary of Religious Terms,"
turned to the marked page
and asked if, in my opinion, the soul
lives on after death. I answered
that it's possible, but no one really knows,
that there are various stories, but I
don't have the time. And I closed the door
like some god
or at least an immortal...

When life has used us up
and we return to the ground, lifting the grass,
and with it into the udders of cows,
then I'll tell them, if I can,
if I don't start thinking,
why would I?...

February, 2013

If I Wasn't a Poet, I'd Be

A burdock by the path
to the outhouse, clinging
to your skirt; a tick
in your groin comfortably infecting
you with Lyme disease;
a pit of hot coals
into which your headdress would fall
and ignite instantly;
a ticking bomb
waiting for the final "tick"...

I would be no one,
for whom oneself does not suffice.
And if I wasn't
no one,
I would be just a poet.

August, 2011

Burning a Life

"Addresses," postcards, greetings,
"for the birth or resurrection of the Most Holy Jesus,"
prescriptions, blood tests, cardiograms,
(I file the letters separately, in the archive),
worn-out and almost new clothes,
dentures, x-rays,
bank cards, receipts,
bouquets of dried flowers (so their shapes,
seeping like smoke through the wall of this world,
would regain their once-possessed bodies
laid by a dead soul's hand
at Persephone's feet),
fear and doubt, dismal sorrow,
feverish prayers
(I need to periodically add wood
so the flame will not suffocate),
poems copied by hand,
mostly banal
(she was not understood, not addressed
in her own language—I lacked the wisdom and love
to cross the distinct imaginings,
vexations and little lies,
learn to keep company
naturally, without pretense),
the poems she wrote,
unskilled but full of passion
(these too—into the archive),
works of art—trifles of mass production,
that moldered unnoticed on the furniture,
and that entire receded time—
days and nights, years,
all full of words, feelings, misunderstandings
and understandings, memories, hopes—
the real life that we cannot enter,
where our bodies are just a precondition.

ZDANYS

She seemed to have wanted cremation,
considered it and changed her mind.
They buried her in the earth.
And I am now cremating
everything she lived with,
what is more than the body,
more than what we are.

December, 2011

Dust

A middle-aged man
has many tiny things
that dust always coats.

As he wipes them, things return
to fields of vision, waken memory, uncover
people's faces, moments of the past.

A middle-aged man has many moments of the past,
settled in oblivion
that wipes away with the dust.

The substances of dust and oblivion are not the same
but both are the products of wear.

And what about things in closets, dressers, drawers!
Only dreams wipe them.

December, 2012

Cleaning the Cistern

I siphoned out a lot of water, cleanly dug
leaves and mud from the bottom of the cistern
my father had framed to collect
    the falling rain.

It hadn't been cleaned since his death,
autumns had filled it with their harvests,
in the meantime I've managed to collect
    a few autumns myself.

How do I scrape out their gathered burden,
rotting deep under the limpid surface
of shallow consciousness, I mused, leaning
    on a pitchfork's handle.

Because night, often changing those dregs
into the images of dreams, tries to tell me
that I have lived through those years like this
    peculiar cistern.

I've submerged everything into myself that fell,
misunderstood the meaning of phenomena,
what I thought I believed, it turned out, were
    masks of desire.

Then the pile of rot suddenly said to me:
there are many useless dregs in you, but perhaps
they might fertilize the furrows of your lines
    if you sow again.

Not a bad idea, I thought, and buried the whole pile
under the young trees in the garden.
Now I only need to wait for the fruits—
    perhaps someone will eat them...

February, 2015

Swamp People

They replaced the mythical creatures of the swamps,
changed themselves into stumps, hummocks, rocks,
sank into quagmires,
fear thickening the air, closing above them
in ferro-concrete contemplation, but did not die.
No one later dug up their remains in the peat bogs,
did not hear death's testimonies
in the witches' perfidious sighs.
They remained alive without breathing,
without quavering the chords of their voices,
they thought quite simply,
and their ferro-concrete mind, enveloping them
like melted reactors,
began to crack on its own, swamp blight
gnawing the railing's sticks, framework. And they got back
their human forms, rose out of swamp quagmires,
did not betray the water and the land, not accommodating
themselves to foreign beliefs.
Sunsets reddened the gentle evening air,
tuned, reconciled the world,
but their time had already passed.
The earth invited them to return.

January, 2016

The Ivory Tower
    (Scenario for a Short Film)

An autumn landscape, morning fog,
a telephone booth on thin wire legs
gets out of sequence, a voice:
hello, I won't describe the world
in terms of my own shadow,
do you hear that, bitch? Give that apple back,
your embers have died inside me, don't rekindle
the wasting fire's reflections.

The telephone booth
lopes out of use.

September, 2012

Fragmentation: Phrygians
(Scenario for a video installation)

Quickly—he shouts—quickly dismantle the monitor,
everyone his part—and into those red bags,
boarding has already begun!
We disconnect smoothly in small sections
and with little bags—to the security control.
Everyone passes, sit on chairs like in garden beds.
Flying into place, easily (quickly, quickly)
we connect the parts again, the operator
pushes the button, but instead of this
well-acted video installation
on the fragmented screen, our heads
sprout wearing red bags
as if Phrygian caps... What's this all about—
the director howls—reload,
take my memory! But turning it on again—
it's the same result—exhausted by commands Phrygian heads,
which are replaced every five minutes
by a charming commercial across the screen
about some sort of winged creatures
and it incites a timid hope that everything will be all right
and eventually the scene we long for will appear...
But no—it's those Phrygians again.
    The audience
has already poured out into the hall. It's a goddess—
a small group
of girls quacks pointing fingers. Then the director
puts his finger to his temple
and shoots himself down.

September, 2012

The Difficulties of Integrating into Society
(Scenario for a Computer Game)

Snowflakes fall lazily,
a dog barks,
its voice sticks the snowflakes into lumps,
snow bombs fall from heaven,
a mouse helps the dog,
it has nine lives
which flow away as a song plays:
    I just wanted to say
    I just wanted to say
    That I live in this yard.
Bump. Want to begin again?

January, 2013

The Prosecutor
(Scenario for the prosecutor's speech)

Whatever we say here and now,
time kills us slowly. Just look:
the defense is trying everything to distract you—
pulls masks over things, takes away
their symbolic meanings, and vice versa—
gives meanings to the accused.
I declare this, as Prosecutor-General. (However,
the defense isn't stupid, tells us that time
does not exist, is rather his own imagining,
an eternal present swallowing its own tail,
and duration is something else entirely,
like the arrow of a dial, an abstraction
that cannot be personified, even if
you manage to put a price on it.
"Thou hast nor youth nor age,
But as it were an after dinner's sleep,
Dreaming on both."—they grab quotes, assemble
authorities, though predatory scavenger-birds
already circle overhead...)
And where will our desires and sufferings go?! I ask.
They can't come up with a timely answer.
So I then move on to the charges—
against things and masks, scavengers.
The past might need to be set free on bail,
and it might even be acquitted,
but for the future I demand at least a hundred years,
postponing punishment until that time.

September, 2015

Stolen Cows
(Scenario for a Defense Summation)

We know, your Honor,
that demons stole the cows.
My client Barabbas is just a gatekeeper
who has an addiction to accumulate and lock up.
I ask for psychiatric expertise!
For if he is judged to be of sound mind,
could we maintain that this is a criminal inclination!
Do we not all have it, including the two of us, your Honor?
Do we share the access to our accounts?
Well, sometimes fools share them.
Don't we lock the doors of our lives?
Well, sometimes fools forget to....
You say he's the demon's accomplice?
But do they choose humans to be their accomplices?
No, they just make use of our human weaknesses.
In that case, the weakness of my defense, your Honor:
to separate oneself and lock oneself up,
to accumulate and not share,
or divide into the good self and the bad other?
You say: he locked up not his own good?
But he is the gatekeeper, he locked the gate.
For him to lock the gate is like grass growing,
like water flowing downward.
Does grass choose where to grow—in a garden or by the road?
It grows wherever the wind carries its seed.
Is there a good and a bad, a proper and an improper wind?
Can we judge someone for his nature?
If so, then according to which article?
Do we have evidence that by locking up the cows
the defendant was seeking some sort of benefit?
Are we going to crucify him as well?...
Just a minute! I've just received a message...
Yes. Saints' prayers crumbled the mountain, freed the cows.
So what sort of door is it, what sort of gatekeepers?!
Merry Christmas, your Honor!
Merry Christmas to all gathered here!

December, 2013

Thimble Dance

Her bulging eyes in a covetous face
watch the dance of three tangled polished thimbles
near the entrance to the market.
Here—she points—and the dextrous fingers of destiny
lift a lid convex as a coffin's—and...empty...
I'm not yet under it, I'm not yet under it!
So the Lady
will need to be satisfied with a more modest supper.
The hundred lives she had pulled out
of her dirty sack
and spattered on the abraded table
disappear in the capacious pocket of forgiveness and love.
(Organs transplanted, donors' blood poured into others,
bone marrow reproclaim
places for living...) And she does not place bets,
she has no more this morning.
The dextrous fingers of destiny itch with satisfaction—
for them—only the gambling,
nothing else matters.

September, 2017

The Art of Love

I

A peasant's son, a shepherd,
each day I saw how animals coupled
in our arcadia, while at mass on Sundays
the strict pastor told us to mortify our bodies,
chase away sinful thoughts that love
can be connected with actions to extend people's
families and is not assigned only to God
or a depersonalized neighbor. Joy,
and where—I thought—is joy,
which every faith should encourage
(even our strict pastor's)
as its most important gift?...
Then I began to pray, asking the virgin martyrs
from the pastor's sermons, especially St. Cecilia,
to teach me the art of love.
I thought—our parishioners,
throwing little fat jokes back and forth,
hush up something important
(perhaps the joy that love could provide),
simulate being those arcadian animals.
But the virgins
loved only Jesus or at least the angels,
did not let earthly men, except for executioners,
touch them, kissed only swords
and axes, bathed in boiling oil.
That seemed a little strange to me:
behind their unconquerable souls loomed
a hard to define borderless corporeality,
like rocks of joy rising
from the waters of many dreams,
only a small portion of which each of us can understand.

II

But Klara was not like that—her gentle body
was embraced by a coarse horsehair shirt under her habit,
she sleeps on dried branches, a wooden log
under her head, her dreams
no, are not wooden, are sweeter than honey,
she sees her lover's face in her dreams,
behind it sail all the gods and demons,
vows of poverty stronger than a rock,
the waves of our oceans do not affect them,
she left this earth at some point,
she will not bear children, her lover
isn't like that, neither is she. It's not easy to understand
because "wisdom does not reach simpletons,
it does not live in the shadow of sin."

III

And what would the hierarchs say from their thrones?
They say: order is established,
and those who stick emotion's bombs under it
are diseased, hysterics, sick with paroxysms of love,
hallucinations. They suffer until they die,
become not dangerous, even cease being apparitions.
Then they are proclaimed saints,
or at least blessed. And while they still live
the best way to deal with them
is to channel their emotions to homeless shelters,
hospitals, oratories, educational institutions,
give them great joy for serving their neighbors,
because that's how two birds are shot:
passionates are employed
and hierarchs affirmed in their posts. And those
who are not suited for work are fenced away
from people by monastery walls,

vows of silence, grow
in happiness under God's watchful eye.
Yes, order is established.

IV

Green sweet flags and duckweeds, dark green grass—
a world I first tried to know—
in the eyes of livestock it all seemed eatable,
just as in my own—desirable,
as she wades through that greenness with a full tureen
back-and-forth each day;
then another takes her place and still another, wrapped
in semblances or contemplations.
And that's how life passes.
It would have been better if I had read books
and lived longer in my imagination,
sinning in thought and word
rather than not sinning at all
rather than not having a reason why.
Black sheep in the chamomile meadow
offer no meaning but do give wool and milk.
With dogs and cows we create a harmonious community
able to subsist and exchange with others,
and that's how we maintain our lives.

I stopped going to church:
what would I be there—an elder of dogs and cows?
What news would I bring back to my community?
That physical love is meant only for continuation of the species?
They know that better than I and the preacher do.
Know that putting the words "love" and "art"
together is a perversion
I would understand better if I had read some books.
Though perhaps it might be possible to link
them to knowledge how to surmount

that distance to happiness, walking by with the tureen,
to the sacrament of marriage and the continuation of the family?
Perhaps not. That's what customs are for,
legal-property relations, position in society.
And who am I? A shepherd. How would art help me?

V

Order is established. And I'm already like a bishop's skeleton
on my heart's throne, hierarch,
hiding my emotions in metal coffers,
closing loves in hanging cages
in the monastery's basements,
a timid shepherd watching how she walks
to and fro like time itself, a gloomy hermit
holding forth in defensive enclosures,
talking to my livestock
in pretentious orations, seeing
how emotions evaporate, joy dries out,
how loves die in those cages from hunger,
saying nothing, accepting their fates,
if there is no other way, only passion,
if there are only shelters, hospitals, oratories,
if there is only the art of love,
if there is no madness, ecstasies, visions
and insights, no happiness,
no angels or holy virgins
wrapped up with the light of heaven,
everything safely removed, reclaimed—
soft bedding, fine linens,
milk baths, bodies pampered
with fragrant oils, an unreal,
unreal life.

The smells of the underground walk among my ribs—
an illusion of life. It's not easy to admit

that all of your past imaginings
were meaningless and wrong, just semblances,
a theater of shadows, showing an invented
drama of life with bones made of plastic
for the purpose of instructing students, borrowed
by a scenographer for this performance.

March, 2016

Satire in Winter

I

Frost dressed the pines as if posing them
for Christmas cards, cold seeps to the bones,
smoke in the cottage presses tears,
eyes veiled by a white film of rime.
Through it I see forest nymphs,
always leading from a distance and, when I turn back,
running away through tender spring meadow grass.
They prowl drowsily among the torpid trees,
Long hair lashing their reddened bodies,
their erect nipples
touch the coarse, frosted bark and again recoil.
Hollow apparitions—
Desire doesn't fill their bodies with the saps of imagination,
Doesn't lend them muscles or bones.
Cold clutches the heart with rough palms.

What floated me into this unpleasant landscape?
Natura? An untamed nature by birth?
I look at the surface of the film of wine—what is it?
And who am I—the fruit of whose imagining?
My fingers cramp around the flute.
But sounds do not stick together
into melody, fall from their own intonations,
not adhered by emotion.

II

How to return to that land of spring
where I lived so long without being there,
imagining myself and imagined by others
in luxuriant, shade-filled landscapes?

Fire crackles in the hearth.
A nymph knocking on the door
(one of those who would run off—
I didn't know them, didn't understand their behavior,
their language, words that meant something else)
sap gushes singing a forest song
until it quiets like a storm outside the window.
Hands stretch idly toward the guide
who warms, then intoxicates, then lulls to sleep
but doesn't say which dream is real, which is not a dream,
how reality extends through sensations to consciousness
and through what it returns again.

III

Out of the landscape run active
shapes of living beings
which earlier I compared to blood
that ignites flames, congealing
to planes of canvas, cold statuary marble,
ornamentalizing, settling with
dust in the mausoleums of things.

The way frost transforms the grass
and trees into wondrous sculptures
is how people's culture pastes
life's flame with death.
That's how time seeps into bones
and fetters the joints, and freezes
me into this kunstkamera
which will now lend only images
to the rampages of the living.

IV

My eyelids are heavy with sleep,
sweet as death, contours of thoughts blend,
other visions rise. Tense, with hope,

I try to touch the edge where the contemplated image
unhooks itself from will and consciousness
like a boat at night from a bent willow
and rocks toward a dream, but I can't grasp it. New
performers creep in but... nothing changes.
Shadows among the trees, streaming hair.
Those filled with life, where are they from?

Are they only images raised by the processes
of food and wine that fill a napping
demigod's animal body?
Or boats lost in a dream
with the remains of memory returning
to some kind of moonlight?

2015

The Poetess' Grave

Here it is more spacious, brighter, in memories,
as if in Persephone's underground kingdom's drawing rooms,
she can leave whenever she wants and return—
the springs of consciousness disregard the sun's seasons.

Though time on the surface flows only in a single direction,
in the depths of the heart many of them begin and end,
may those meadows all blossom with the shadows of flowers,
may they not extend themselves with the bodies of frenzied life.

Who you visit in words, who you appear to, having taken
your former shape with smiles, glowing glances,
the softness of your skin—you call us all to catharsis.

Those will pass quickly, and the others for a time will delight
in the ripples of sense from sounds to the shores of shape,
until wordless meanings drape across your forgotten grave.

September, 2010

Anniversary

Words tangle in my mouth—I need a rhythm—
there's nothing to talk about.

She climbs like a screw around the axle of consciousness,
appears on the left, disappears on the right.

Her heart appropriates my rhythm
and there are no words in my mouth.

And I'm here with flowers for her, jasmine,
it's the season now, and each blossom—

not rhythm in a mouth heavy with words
but lips open for a kiss.

It's a rhythm all the same, though so slow
that it can't be adapted to music.

Kisses of memory are buried in crypts,
the rhythmical tongue in my mouth

arranges words
around them.

June, 2010

Bicycles in the Garage

There are as many as seven bicycles in the garage:
the "Minsk" was my father's, gone twelve years now,
the "Baltik Vairas," that I received from the journal *Varpas*
as a literary prize back when bicycles were already
not my preferred means of transportation,
the "Terminator" was my young son's, my wife's "Panther,"
all of them made in Šiauliai, like myself, and three others—
my grandchildren's, some too big, some too small…
Sometimes someone rides them,
pumping up the tires, sometimes I try to ride one
as I used to do, when the tires pumped themselves up
from inspiration, or the pressure of necessity…

Memories—yes. They ride
the curbs of clouds, fall into oblivion,
appear again (from over the mountain, as Blake wrote).
Maybe that's why I don't throw them away. I can't.
Because they are the shadows of those bicycles,
the childish, the youthful, and the adult ones,
on which I rode, they say, with cold passion,
though I would say with hot wonder.

I constantly visit them,
just like the other lodgers of this garage
that I will never need, dispense warm glances to each.
I know no one will steal them, even if I leave the gates unlocked.
I don't know what awaits them…

March, 2016

Sixty-Year-Old Women

It's spring again, the chestnuts have blossomed,
and they are the same as in those other spring times,
waiting for radiant glances, words sticky with pollens,
a bit distorted on the muddied screen of time,
and no, as before, somewhat shy, not wanting to think
what will happen after this whiteness fallen to the ground.
Souls like blossoming plum trees (even, sometimes, in autumn)
in sterile reflected-contemplated gardens:
sighs that were and weren't, imaginary bees of smiles
visit and weighed down fly with the wind to oblivion.
Mirrors don't reflect the truth and the scales lie.
They sink ever more often and deeper into themselves leaving
the flat world to bloom its moments: they blossom
much more steadily, as in paintings or poems.

May, 2011

July. Ikebana.

The hot days
at last have ended. It rains
sometimes. A thought like a boat in a puddle,
carried my way but drifting past.
I cling to summer's throat
with teeth blue with berries or wine...

Tamarisk, yellowed day lily,
lotus leaf, reddish water lily,
smoke tree. The boat has reached
the shore. You are not in it.
You are in the bouquet's memory.

July, 2015

Safe Rendezvous

Walking past the fig tree we picked fruit
with so many tiny seeds.

Back at the hotel we made love
listening to furniture being moved, footsteps—
overheard phrases echoing in our conciousnesses.
When we drank coffee on the terrace,
lives had passed, and all
circumstances had safely returned
to their places, while warehoused experiences
lost the threat of rising factors.

July, 2015

The Carp

It's as cramped here as a supermarket—on both sides of the glass
two crowds of the condemned rub their flanks.

She stabbed with her finger and said: I want that one.
The saleswoman began to mix the
the aquarium's suffocating water with a ladle.

I tried to twist away, that's why the fishing took time,
but the finger's stinger already stuck into my heart.

I thrashed in the oxygen's abundance and gasped
pulled out into unfamiliar air
thinned by my own desires.

Then the saleswoman stuck me
into a plastic bag—this world's
invisible but sealed border pressed tight.

For a moment I still imagined how her graceful fingers
would separate my bones from soft braised flesh,
how I will let myself go across those dreamed lips
into the hungry grave in her belly.

July, 2010

Naiad

I

Having gone more than half the way, I found myself
in a withering forest filled with spider webs.
Parting their sticky threads I saw
a young woman with a gloomily shining face.
In the thickets, the depths, near a clear brook.
A small waterfall fell on her belly, she washed her breasts
with soft hands and, it seems, in the corner of her eye
saw me before I saw her,
but did not run, did not hide, as she always did. I
stood frozen, bewitched by her beauty, having stepped
into a different world through Arachne's barely visible net,
then I drew closer, held her by her shoulders, turned her around,
dived into her eyes, into memory, and pressed against
the clear water's vagueness,
against its fluid knowledge, floating souls to oblivion,
and two streams merged.
I felt how the desiccated crystals of my thoughts
were melted and augmented by the liquid world's Sofia,
how I talk to her liquidly and receive liquid response,
I don't know if I'm still a man or an ocean mammal,
don't know if I will ever be allowed to know,
but believed sacredly I had not waded into that same river.
And so: the river stands here still, as it had always stood,
even the small waterfall is congealed in the air.

II

My throne is in a shady wood at the bottom of a brook,
strewn with small stones, soft as velvet,
twelve springs flow together there and merge into one
so it would flow freely to me, past me and into the distance,
where it will widen, deepen, turn into a river. And here I
rule my region, district, saps and souls.

And so a faun sneaks up, with his foot splashes
one of the springs, I notice, when his desire rises,
but I stop him with my hand, the brave spirit obeys,
stands, and with a fiery look swallows my flowing will,
the brook's water bubbles up, the springs begin to boil
until a sudden rain pours down, and with the tiniest drops
washes over me from head to toe,
even a rainbow manages to shine for a moment—a sign
that the heavens have given the ruler of springs this power.

May, 2017

A Strange Flower

The carriage gently rocks my body and so, finally, my home,
on the shore—neoclassic, Doric columns,
and a terrace with a marble parapet hanging above the ocean...
I walk through the door and in the anteroom on a table—
a fragrant letter in a gilded envelope with a coat of arms.
In it is written that the awaited guest is arriving,
I've heard a great deal about him, am impatient to see him.
My pulse quickens, I go straight out to the terrace, it's quiet,
there's barely a wave on the ocean. Suddenly
I feel a man's hand on my shoulder, see the other in front of me,
offering me a strange never seen before flower—a flexible
slightly prickly long stem, and its blossom like some sort of bulb.
I accept the gift but am afraid to turn around:
and what if it isn't the one I was waiting for?
The hand that gave the flower descends
onto my other shoulder and moves my dress off of it,
the flower drops from my hand into the water, I can't
take my eyes away as if I was casting a spell: if it sinks
it will be one way and if it floats far away another...
And I don't notice that I am already naked, though I touch
his gentle fingers forgetfully, hesitate to turn around, just climb
out of the enchanted circle of my dress that has fallen to my feet,
I rest my chin and elbows on the parapet and feel him inside me,
still don't dare to turn around, though I can feel his legs, then
have a clever idea: if I bent over as if turning to a sheaf, looked
at him from the bottom so our eyes did not meet ... And I do that,
and see that there is no visitor, there's no one there,
not even the flower on the water... Was it?

September, 2017

Dream Thief

I pass through eyelash gates
with the night fog and touch
the soft surface of dreams. No,
her feet can't be allowed to so avidly
touch that soft desert of fine sands,
canals of water in it, coiling
like tiny snakes, she can't be allowed
to feel it with her palms, to smooth or dig
a small hole from which she could drink. She
can't be allowed. That's why I ask her to dance, music
coming as if from nowhere, my face beneath a mask.
That doesn't bother her, we dance passionately,
her long hair billows
and brushes against my deeply cowering face,
and I suddenly turn into a doll, like a large robot,
which twitches, tries to move awkwardly.
She's annoyed that I stole a dance from her dream.
I'm annoyed that I suddenly lost my body.
She takes my clumsy hand and tries
to put it on her shoulder, but the doll doesn't react
to it or to the music, she is lost in the dream,
she can't leave it, she doesn't know through where.
And the guards draw near, their swords rattle.
What face will they put on me when they lock
me up with the long chains of her hair?
With what face will I appear to her in gates
of elephant ivory or ordinary bones?

April, 2017

The Rose Tunic

I had not yet been merged though I knew, felt,
how such a thing happens. That lake stretched in me,
clear and transparent, without rushes, almost
like the one Ovid wrote about...
Yes, I had loved before then, had already
reached half a century...

We sat at the table then having buried our grandmother—
relatives and friends. And he across from me, unclear where
he came from, a handsome young man, much younger,
looked like some sort of foreigner. There was a look then,
piercing, unreadable, different than those of men
who had looked me up and down before. Passionate?...
Probably passionate. He asked my name,
and with a somewhat trembling voice I answered: Salmacis.
He didn't react at all. He asked where I lived
and offered to walk me home. I felt
how my breast was pierced by emptiness,
able to accept him...
I had not yet been merged though I knew, felt,
how such a thing happens. A lake...
He was not outside the window or was inside me.
What would I do with him—a thought flashed—would
I give birth to children?
Then I told the young man I didn't have time, was hurrying
to the amphitheater where I was rehearsing
some sort of rituals, while with my joints I felt
thick ropes that, it seems, the city's residents
had firmly wound around me...
That's why I stood to leave...

He grabbed me by the waist on the porch and turned me around.
I almost collapsed, my legs felt weak.
I walked like a puppet pulled by strings, my body not obeying me.
Later I wandered a long time as if in a dream, searched for him,

inquired of the people who had been there. But to no avail.
Perhaps he went abroad. I probably wouldn't know him
now if I saw him again... I bought then
a rose tunic, rose sandals...

And for a long time I walked as if in a dream, all in rose,
those I met told me my face was glowing.
I thought: what if he jumped into a clear lake,
into the emptiness in my breast, and I after him, and we
had merged into one. Forgetting our names,
those held by the ropes that wound us...

My rose tunic illuminated a gloomy world
and made the gods smile. Touching myself
still for a long time, I saw his look before my eyes,
imagined how he disappeared suddenly under the table
as if beneath the mirror of a lake,
not noticed by others,
how bodies droop in the warm waters,
souls melt in them, merge into one...

Was that love, or just
desire, passion, a spark, Aphrodite, yours,
not managing yet to ignite it?

January, 2017

Monument

We didn't notice the fracture, we thought—
a strand of a goddess's hair had fallen, chisels governed
by computers sculpting this perfect copy of Myron,
not from marble but from granite. And so—
setting it on its pedestal the monument split
into two pieces and almost crushed me,
just managed to break the bones of my foot.

It's in a cast now, doesn't look
like part of a marble sculpture,
some kind of inept thing, more the packing
than the packaged,
and really—not winged...
Perhaps that hair really is a goddess's?
So she fractures
destinies and forces us to choose—obey,
leave our usual routines (with these crutches?)
our assumed shapes, or dream further
cowering in a mouse's burrow...
A simple fracture,
unnoticed, unexpected...

December, 2016

Foxwoods Casino

Once again you haven't found that path, didn't notice
the crack in the panorama of images—the Lama says. No doubt.
I'm not a born gambler, don't see the purpose
(or am afraid?) to take the risk, to throw the chip
into the domain of blind chance.
Because what I can win in this casino—
just the slavery of not belonging to myself,
attachments and the tearing of tethers,
meaningless torments and rebukes of conscience.
Foxes from these woods (piercing looks,
naked arms, shoulders and backs)
pretend they are waiting for a simple presentation,
radiant smiles never vanish from their lips
when I put down the bought chip—
it's just the beginning. But I play on
using change, win sometimes, sometimes not.
The foxes' glances are carried off on the roulette wheel
until wind blows the smiles one-by-one from their lips.
We understand that same game differently—I say—
putting down on the red and the black, for me it's the end
in itself, such pleasures are not sufficient for you.
You could win a real life—
the woman next to me at the table says angrily—you can
imagine it, and the bewitched souls of the players
would follow you like a piper down paths of glory.
Haven't you had enough of this musty little life,
of these callous, dreary intercourses—she says. Excusing myself
for a minute I turn past the suddenly revealed exit door.
The Lama says nothing.

March, 2015

Journey's End

Everything is already said, suitcases stacked
in the cabin's corner. Pack up,
pack up your cosmetics, hygienic necessities
(she as always will forget something).
Memory does not fit,
the lids will not close—let's leave them
let those shadows hang like ghosts
in fluttering poems.

We climb out of bed,
and the endless dream
meets the shore.

October, 2011

The Tarnishing Mirror

I took it out of my grandparents' wardrobe with all the doors
and stood it up in the attic, and I burned the wardrobe—
it just took up space and did not accommodate the things
that had accumulated over the years—unnecessary
dreams, perceptions, imaginations. The mirror—
I remember my grandmother said—is the door to another room
that looks the same, only somewhat parallel,
more dependent on reflective consciousness.
Those doors are everywhere now—the bathroom, the bedroom, the hallway,
in them only private meaningless sleepy faces,
as if they don't know where they are. And the tarnishing mirror
is something else—visions of another room have already begun
to fade in it—dark spots slowly
expand, testify to time, melt the line
between expropriated realities, darkening their spells...
I wait until that boundary is as tarnished as the mirror,
and at the last moment perhaps my real face will find its contours
like the currents of Lethe... Look—she says from there—
how beautifully this world shines,
and with that jabbering you only confuse and waste
precious tarnishing time.

February, 2020

Praying Mantis

> *The truth of poetry is a scandal. A thousand naked*
> *fornicating couples with their moans and contortions*
> *are nothing compared to a good metaphor*
> Charles Simic

You no longer have the time to sing sadly—she said,
the woman, who makes, then considers, the spinner—
time for you to turn into a beetle according to the consequences
that you summoned by so casually treating
the reflections of the world, though you considered that it exists,
made yourself insignificant, hidden, self-doubting,
confusing catharses with orgasms, ecstasies...
All right—I said—I'll become a praying mantis,
a zealous visitor of monastery nurseries and gardens,
taking on the same social status
in the food chain of insects.
At least a female or an elephant's foot...

No one escapes change. My dead father,
who always tried to protect me
from a woman-spinner who makes, then reconsiders,
asks from behind the cloak of a dream: will you still write
your happiest verses? I find it strange:
such a serious man, reading those obscenities,
yet pushing the libertine
into the mire of metaphors.

August, 2019

Metaphysics

> *Philosophy is not one of the natural sciences.*
> *(The word "philosophy" must mean something*
> *whose place is above or below the natural*
> *sciences, not beside them.)...*
> *Philosophy is not a body of doctrine but an activity.*
> Ludwig Wittgenstein, *Tractatus Logico-Philosophicus*, 4.III, 4,112

I.

My soul is somewhat corpulent, but its anthropomorphic
proportions are sufficiently attractive, it wears or drags a white
slightly tight dress which, at this moment,
has managed to cover its top half and buttocks.
I say "at this moment" because if philosophy is not
doctrine but activity, then perhaps metaphysics is action?
So the anthropomorphic God (let it be in capital)
and my soul flutter together and that white dress
exactly now weaves itself metaphysically
from top to bottom, and the thread stretches from God's cloak
that unravels from bottom to top, ever clearer to Him
as the metaphysical gaze opens...
(Moralists, calm yourselves — He has girded his loins.)
You ask, why is this moment to wit portrayed here?
Right, I would very much not want to bare that soul,
so Eros would not seep in through decorative junctions
and would not begin to disturb the action, distort the artistic image.
This process would be better expressed by some mathematician,
describing the given moment of the state of the dress-cloak
using a formula, even some kind of binomial,
though that would be an external scheme of the image, not mine —
significance without meaning, lost or not fully opened
protecting themselves from outside significances. So they would offer
no benefit either to science (if philosophy stands above or below
but not alongside it), nor to metaphysics (perhaps it, too —
above or below but not alongside philosophy?) So

imagination carries out the work somewhat more simply and easily
and prevents us from diving into metaphysical action,
e.g., to so intimately associate with God—
across the thinnest thread of life.

2.

And later, once, at some moment,
as if the player's tape reversed itself on its own,
the thread moves ahead, but now in the other direction: the dress
begins to unravel itself from the bottom to the top, opening
its grayed, time-abused body to the empirical gaze
(ah, it's not necessary to address the eternal present,
imagined time, just look into mirrors),
while God's cloak weaves itself from the top to the bottom,
misleading the metaphysical gaze again in liturgical pleats
as if the power of life is in aesthetic images...
And that's how you long to leave it all to mathematics.
Because we understand what will happen when the thread of life
somewhere near the neck will snap from the nonexistent dress.
I don't know what will happen to the soul then, where it will go,
if it, or something hers, will repeat a similar
process, ask the priests or
let's leave it to metaphysics.

December, 2020

St. Jerome's Apologia

The lion and the skull. Sun and sand.
What is unnecessary leaves consciousness, evaporates, seeps
into the desert of Antioch, the body dries, the soul clarifies,
the mind sharpens, and hard particles settle in letters waiting
for other eyes, their light and life, to turn into new images,
meanings, perceptions. Forty days later,
Moses comes down from Sinai with tablets of stone.
People who went through the desert following a snake-flag
asked Aaron to cast for them an image of God
from earrings and necklaces,
and he cast a golden bull, the old, normal symbol
in these countries, with a sun disk between its horns,
who floated Europa to Crete in the foggy future
perhaps standing meekly by the manger...
(No, we will not mention Pasiphaë here or the sonorous copper.)
That's why Jerome gives Moses horns as if inviting
us to a cozy and peaceful settled civilization, to civil law,
the cool density of olive trees and vines. But no,
he breaks the symbol with the blocks of his law, the blocks—
into the symbol—will have to return to the mountain.
There will be no peace, blood will flow for millennia.
Drunk from him and gold, let us spread knowledge, what we do not know.
Gods will shed their horns like deer and grow them again, as we,
passers-by, will need to give up our short lives for promised eternity.
False prophets will explain everything to us honestly.
And we will continue to make translation mistakes, foremen.
In the cathedral niche, Moses again with sprouting horns.

August, 2020

Heavenship

We built a kind of heavenship
in which we intended to fly to a Christian heaven,
it came out looking like a church steeple,
but as we finished it collapsed, why, we do not know.
As if the earth shook, or some other finger of God
flicked it down. The cabin into
the rocket's booster stage. It took a long time to scratch
it out of there. Some Hindus, toiling alongside
(I don't remember their names), were quite kindhearted,
offered to make a cart from what was left
(a doubtful enough attitude toward new technologies),
on which we would get to almost where we were headed.
Those remains seemed to us
not suitable for anything, so we said—do what you want.
And they built three of them, in fact, and now
we walk around those carts, hands pressed to our sides,
looking as if at works of art made from second-hand
materials, in a new context having gotten new meaning,
and think—to which gallery of contemporary art
should we offer them?

October, 2018

Showfee

I remember how my grandmother taught me to pray
to St. Cornelius, my protector,
and I had almost learned those prayers,
but she would not let me say them, because when I began:
"Saint Cornelius, showfee..."
Don't say that—she would scold me—"showfee"!
Why not say that? If he's not a showfee
why should I pray to him at all? What is he,
if not a showfee? A centurion?
What is that centurion? In the end I got angry
and said terrible things about God,
and she stopped teaching this devil spawn. And later,
when I became World Beauty's chauffeur,
I wanted to be at least a centurion. I drove
her up and down changing altitudes and would truly
have apologized to my grandmother and to offended God,
but she was no longer in the world and I didn't know God. Beauty
said to me that I look more like an elevator operator, and He
might have forgotten that incident. The brakes broke,
the guard rails didn't work, I rolled into my childhood,
where the centurion walks with the chauffeur holding the beauty,
staggering a bit, undoubtedly a little drunk.

October, 2018

Toward Home

She didn't promise me immortality, she promised
a long life full of adventures, like a film
flickering in your eyes, even with 25th cadres—
gentle and imperceptible slavery, a blind
wall of imagination which—I knew—sooner or later
would break through with cudgels of questions and doubts.
The migrants' boat was waiting on Libya's shore, I had
bought myself a place on it—a participant in the war,
or perhaps a criminal (who here now would know?). Home,
which might be longing for me—how real
and tangible is it? How real and tangible
have we remained?

Waves will rock me as they rocked me
not concerned if I am real, if I exist at all.
Some dog might be able to affirm that,
if such a dog still exists somewhere.

November, 2019

Phantom of the Opera

Those remote little people with my name and last name,
the tribe of nobody's land, settling in memory
in the theater basement among unused decorations—
what do they do there, perhaps suffocate with their oblivion?
One or two of them somehow crawl up on stage at night,
begin singing half-remembered arias, voices breaking,
try to recreate their most famous roles,
to justify, demonstrate, that their art was a mature one—
and so many flowers and applause in the orchestra and balconies,
and so what if the audience had forgotten them long ago,
and only the ghosts of dreams now go to the opera—
they applaud artists equally well in the dark footlights.
They call me out as well, and I need to listen to them,
thinking that I might correct the basement soloists' mistakes,
if I rewrote into verse their boring old arias
and they wouldn't force themselves onto the stage at night?
I pour myself a glass of whiskey and smoke a cigarette,
finally forcing the curtain to come down this way.

August, 2019

Mimesis

> *Because artists imitate men in action, these men*
> *must be either of a higher or a lower type*
> Aristotle, *Poetics II*

I agree, Your Honor: plagiarism is bad,
but in our case, these are most likely reproductions, created
so more of our public could become familiar with the originals,
that is, with cultural, educational, touristic goals. The prosecutor said
that they are difficult to distinguish. I ask you please hold
this high assessment as a mitigating factor. For us, artists,
the world is usually not especially friendly—
we remain misunderstood, though we seek understanding...
That this is my case... Yes, a plagiarist—that's bad,
but here he is part of the performance. The essence is the action itself,
the explication of socio-economic relationships, mimesis,
so important to and characteristic of the very nature of art.
Money—a contractual value, having no innate value,
only that established by the federal bank
and culminating with the state. So the bank replicates
originals, whose distinctive traits—banknote numbers—
maintain their nominal relationship with purchasing power
and level of inflation. I tried to imitate this action,
seeking to attract the attention of the honorable public
to the similarities and differences. The extent of a work of art
is limited, that's why its influence on purchasing power is symbolic.
(Would a million escalate inflation?) This increase
is part of artistic action which only clarifies the fact
that the sum of money in circulation depends on the total
of goods and services and not on those holding power, so
we are all subordinate to money, perhaps excepting high art.
If that is in fact the case should be demonstrated by the end
of this process, your decision, Your Honor!

December, 2020

The Tracked Down

> *Turning around I saw my footprints—*
> *One foot a man's, the other a bird's.*
> *"The Followed"*

And sobered I noticed nothing,
well, at least someone's pacing
single foot having stepped in dog shit,
not disposed according to the directions
of town government. Walked in a crooked line:
footprints on the sidewalk, in the stairwell,
on the rug by the door...
Ringing. It's you, Anubis,
shitting in public places?—

No, that's the police officer.
Citizen, do you have a dog?

The gods never answer.
You do that for them.

September, 2009

Field of Vision

She returned back to the egg, which had
already fossilized, became smooth and polished as granite,
and only at the very top a small fountain spouting
directly at her, as she straddled the pointed end,
betrays me—a pliant current of water,
streaming like will-o-the-wisp, spreading
over a strange field of vision. Arms like seaweed
lift from below, slide across the stone's surface,
stretch toward us as if from a different world,
until they grow into the stone and evaporate
creating an intaglio.
Wrinkles carve themselves into the faces.

Once, when I was four, a truck
didn't make it into my field, rolling down our street,
paved with round stones, and knocked me down.
But I remained between its wheels. I crawled out and ran home,
straight toward my grandmother's horror-stricken face.
I felt guilty for running suddenly into the street.
I don't know what governs our
fields of vision, what fills them with things,
what sprouts beauty into our consciousness
and what gods keep us on the side of the seeing.

I didn't dare desire her.
Thought such beauty was not for me,
And so she—a stone,
like all time that has run past.

July, 2018

The Magic Flute

The sound stretched like skeins of fog in the dark
and imperceptibly slithered into ear shells. Five
hungry souls appeared, deeply cowering within themselves.
I was already undivine,
like some Indra after a thousand years, the flute
like a whistle in some goop's hands. A humanlike faun,
fettered by time. We danced in the forest clearing
while the full moon shined, three of us,
because two had left affected by the gravity of earth,
not finding the god because he was already gone,
and then another dropped out, fell,
tripping on herself. Two of us remained, moonlight
settled deep into black pupils and invited us
to return to the pleasant oblivion of Arcadian summers,
to the forest clearing, where peace and harmony melt
the hammered armor of desire and disappointment,
and the wish to give smothers the hunger to get.
We danced giddily across all of congealed time,
rose into the ether and fell into the abyss,
saw in her eyes the smiling goddess,
but the earthly woman closed
her lids and lowered the thick gates of her lashes
remaining within herself. I knew I had to return
even with a step of that dance into Kimmeria's foggy autumn.

September, 2018

The Tree of Knowledge

There is a full alley of trees—it's hard to recognize the real one
but I feel it at once—bashful, as if hiding behind its withered
leaves and covering its fruits, coiled as spirals.
I embrace its trunk, press against it, begin to climb upwards...
Ah, how rigid and soft its branch! I sit down,
pressing my ear listen to how those fruits ring
like quiet bells and awaken desire,
and my body melts, turns to wood. My fingers touch the hollow,
from it pour liquids like a drizzling rain, and that tree, sweetened,
catches it and stretches out its reviving leaves. Then it seems
some sort of flying thing, bird-not-bird, not angel,
bodiless, almost as transparent as a hologram,
carries a large round fruit on its wings.
Not of this tree, it hovers in the air, rises and drops
with the beating of the wings, and seems to glow.
Suddenly its skin tears and its juices begin to drip
on my head, my chest and back, flow down my body,
find the proper path...
And I am pregnant with knowing there is no nonexistence,
or it is right here and now—in perfect ecstasy.

December, 2017

Pythia

I come to her with a baked chicken and a bottle of good wine,
she asks about me, and after eating and a few drinks
she begins to mutter under her breath:
I am you, I-am-you, I-amyou, Iamyou...
The vapor is good today, good vapor, so thick,
intoxicating from the very depths like a resilient snake
writhes into my body, floods my brain,
pulls off the umbilical cord that links me to semblance,
consciousness melts in ecstasy, the many fuse into one.
Therefore this:
I see—you guide that man through swamp-not-swamp, reach
the island in the sea of bog blueberries, in the center of the sphere
he lays you down in the grass, all around flowers-
not-flowers, like eyes, waving on thin stalks,
watching you and glittering like diamonds,
when glances meet... And the sky is like a mirror,
the top half of the sphere, convex, where those flowers
and stars are reflected, and four symbols, like wreathes
arranged in a square, are curdled as cheese and turned
into unrecognizable letters. You sort of know
what they mean, but concepts outstrip intellect. That man
lifts you in his arms toward the symbols, touched,
they begin to shine, guide your finger among them
as if writing something—perhaps the baked chicken recipe?
The universe contracts into a skull. We are dizzy with ignorance.
I am you, I-am-you, I-amyou, Iamyou...
Do we have more wine?

May, 2019

Mermaid

She stumbled across me on the sea shore
sleeping and dreaming, the earth's daughter,
pulled me in like a vortex, pressed against me like water,
her eyes shined with desire, her green hair
spread across my consciousness, her tail caressed my face...
I felt that she thought I was someone else,
called me by another's name, invited me into her element,
but I knew, I said to her, that I would not
survive there without air, and the name....
I will be who she imagines me to be — passion
dissolves forms, transforms one into another...
The taste of the sea on my lips, the rustling of gull wings
as if we were flying through the air...

Suddenly she said she could not bear
being without water and had to return
to her own element and disappeared. I lay on the sand
like an empty barrel rolled out by the waves
thinking: no, this could not be a dream,
but could I even now be awake? ...

Though we became one another, we could not
manage to remain in foreign worlds
longer than a moment of passion.
Stories I'd heard would not help — butterflies
quietly flutter their wings as if they did not exist.
Perhaps only dreams will help. To never waken.

August, 2018

From CONVERSATIONS WITH LI PO
  about mututally pleasant things

The Great Autumn Moon

We drove during the day silent in a car.
It was Friday, the 13th , She was just preparing to rise,
words, expressed long ago, outlined by the mind's
artificial light, others sinking slowly into the mash
of the swamp's quagmire create strange constellations.
Starting to speak she rejoiced in the fall, its colors, the world,
that she loved so much and in which—understand—my
menacing shadow does not loom. I didn't know how to respond…
And at night She rose as she did a million years ago, empty,
as if She had not absorbed so many glances and so much poetry,
I had already drunk wine, so was able
to look at her worshipfully, call her goddess, though I could
see no semblance on her face, only the madness of all
of us who look at her, who looked. I wanted to dance
but had no partner—my shadow wasn't real—
fell from the street lamp (a pollution of light). I could not
in this way disdain the classic. I returned to my room,
to consciousness flooded with moonlight.

September, 2019

Masks

In the Panda city of Chengdu near Tu Fu's house,
your friend's, too thin from sorrow and poetry writing
(you liked him very much—were close, shared
a blanket, walked arm-in-arm)—the Chinese circus
in my day—three performers danced
masterfully alternating masks. I did not understand
how they did that—in the blink of an eye becoming
monsters, dragons, girls or something else.
I was bewitched by their art.
I don't know if you've learned anything from them
because that sort of trade is not essential for us,
if the very words with which we dance are masks,
we change them easily and don't change them,
become what we want to be not becoming anything,
we are that and we are not that, dancing
in our own rhythm and not, do not cover meanings
that emerge with masks, or, on the contrary, try
to alternate them as much as possible during a single dance.

August, 2019

The Temple on the Hill

I climbed a long time but was not admitted
through the heavy gates whose creaking
pierced the heart. I was sorry
I was not a mute dyslexic—I said
too many words about things
I did not know, did not understand.
I offended gods
and demons with my namings.
The guards at the gate were afraid that I'd start talking
rather than plucking stars out of the heavens, Li Po—
that with my voice I'd disrupt the silence, a monk—
that I'd learn the language of bats and beetles
and become their regent.
Mute, I looked at peach orchards in the valley,
at smoke rising from huts like my own thoughts, lost
among the ripening fruit. A stranger in a strange land.

July, 2019

In A Boat of Spice Wood

Flutes encrusted with diamonds, gold horns,
expensive wood under the girls' buttocks,
they sing in soft skin-shivering voices,
the jug of wine turns the heads of listeners.
Free as a merman I follow the gulls with my eyes,
the hills shake with the pounding of the keyboard,
the lovelies tremble with legs pressed shut,
a poem is born, wider and deeper than the sea.
Poetry is immortal! The poet's glory drowns out
the moon and sun and the palaces of rulers collapse...
The income isn't much, but splendor and beauty
surround us, and rivers flow sometimes the other way.

April, 2019

Shadow

Is it me, staggering some other meanings,
not arranging the canon of hymns, not classifying styles,
not drinking so much wine in thick autumn moonlights,
not leaving my cozy home and going to the mountains,
not sitting at the emperor's table, not writing lines drunk,
(angry eunuchs didn't pour water on my face),
not experiencing exile, not asking permission to return,
not mastering the art of fencing and not cutting those enemies,
not marching so many miles and swimming down rivers,
not loving women with vermilion-reddened cheeks,
not abandoning wives and children in distant provinces?
I apologize for the shadow badly mimicking my movements,
a bit late after so much time, space and fancies—
the moonlight's to blame here, or is it me intruding in it?

August, 2019

The Naturalist's Resurrection

> *The great slime kings*
> *Were gathered here for vengeance and I knew*
> *That if I dipped my hand the spawn would clutch it.*
> Seamus Heaney. *Death of a Naturalist*

After six decades I returned here—green frog-spawn
separated both worlds and sweet-flag swords
waved in the wind. Did they think I had died?
Perhaps only forgotten, laid out in unfamiliar moments
with a suit and tie, as is the custom
in that assumed culture, but never forgetting
that uncertainty and fear, that strange disquiet
as the summer air trembles in the heat of the sun,
and repulsive calmness, from which something unknown
might come, the fear to ask and not answer,
wanting to run away knowing it will not succeed.
Stable imaginings walking along an unstable border.
He won't disappear. He resurrects sooner or later
in order to plunge into the unknown again.

June, 2020

To Autumn

It is only your beginning. I see they've rested a while—
trees, vegetables and flowers. Lazily
ripen their fruits, their hidden seeds, and wait
until they will separate from them. There's no enthusiasm,
with which we all squirt spring. But I'm tired of marching
step by step with time. And the fruits have separated,
scattered, most of them seedless. Only the seasons
seem meaningful, conversations about the weather,
vitally important to vegetables...

The second circle's winds rage as they raged,
each season's winds, unavoidable in their own ways,
carrying our emotions, though often only words
and perhaps the thoughts behind them, but I'm not able
to catch those thoughts—they're too quick or too weak,
or don't pay attention to the season, don't have a *kigo*,
though *gathering swallows twitter in the skies.*

September, 2018

The Sitters

I like to sit under that apple tree,
though its fruits rot before ripening.
Once one of them banged the top of my head.
No, no laws of nature or deductions.
I bought a chain saw and wait for fall.
In its place I'll plant a nut tree—
its fruits are smaller, though I'll probably not see
them or its shade.

Ma'am, you also liked sitting under my quill.
Did you replace your equipment?
Or is it still the same scythe?

August, 2018

Swifts

A screeching band appeared as if from nowhere
and attacks the starlings' birdhouse,
in which sit fledglings not yet able to fly.
They're swifts, black spindles of the skies,
much like fighter planes. The starlings try to defend
themselves for a time, but in the end move out.
The swifts take over the home and brood,
and furnish food flying in escadrille.

I went out onto the mansard balcony near that birdhouse.
I visited there rarely. The escadrille
didn't like that—whistled past my head like bullets,
demonstrating that I had transgressed their private space
and must step aside immediately...

And once, a swift fell in the yard, pressing its chest
and wings against the house, stiffened, seized by terror,
so weak and surrendered that my neighbor
wanted to help it but didn't know how.
I understood swifts a little so told him
that these could not lift themselves from the ground
and needed to be picked up and thrown into the air.
I didn't want to touch it myself, had some hard feelings
toward its relatives because of my starlings. I had hard feelings
for the changing world, for myself or for us both. My neighbor
picked it up carefully, not fully believing me,
and threw it upwards so that it would at least fall on the roof
if it didn't fly, but that swift's wings suddenly caught the air
and it managed to return to the escadrille's formation.

July, 2018

Bindweed

My parcel of land, garden, life.
Statutes protect them from bipedals like me.
The bindweed there, where it grew, became unnecessary
so I decided to destroy it because I felt it wouldn't
be enough just to pull it out, I'd have to find its obstinate,
intrusive tentacles of roots weaving like snakes
through cracks in the concrete and bricks, diving, rising
back into the soil. I cut off the shoots,
ripped them off the roof of the woodshed, tore roots
from the ground with my hands and tools, just as stubbornly
(like two women clodding under the surface of appearances)
I overcame it, dug out the roots (because that's the simple
right of the stronger, no matter who decided that),
spreading myself like bindweed on neighboring shoulders,
on apprehension, language and the statutes it expresses,
on property rights, policies, bank accounts
and on every other emptiness, extending the long tentacles
of my roots toward it... watching dolefully
how time tears away my vines from those I love,
how the once supple tissues harden and congeal,
how the tentacles of will contract, return where they came from,
and the one who comes to uproot me will probably
not perspire so profusely nor chatter without reason as much.

March, 2019

The Sowers of Seeds

> *The desert in the garden the garden in the desert*
> *Of drouth, spitting from the mouth the withered*
> *apple seed.*
> T. S. Eliot, Ash Wednesday, V.

It's not my will, not my desire, I don't even know why
I sow seeds all around, because if one sprouts
I smother that shoot, fight with it at the root.
I myself am not able move, have grown into the earth,
that's why I ripen fruits and, as I have been inculcated,
tempt them with couriers—animals, birds, and humans—
to swallow them and throw them away in heaps of manure
as far from me as possible. And it seems I knew something,
though I would need and hunger to satisfy them somehow…
But I don't have, don't know why there are fruits at all,
after frenzied blossoming breaking my joints.

I have desires and imagine I satisfy them.
But the fruits fallen at my feet don't fascinate me.
We have an infrastructure to spread my seeds,
technical conveyances. I have a voice and the couriers' feet,
I haven't spread out my roots and don't jut my branches,
but I don't know what will grow from those seeds if they end up
in wilderness gardens, if most of them are mirages,
if they're not spit out by a desert of drought in a garden
desiccated by beliefs, the earth gnawed by erosion,
if they're not spit out by my embittered mouth
into the counterfeit fruit's dead heart,
what the snake once named as knowledge.

March, 2019

The Wooden Duck

The pond is overgrown with duckweed,
in the middle a duck floated as if roosting
on green ice or carpet. I, a pure-blooded spaniel,
bred to hunt them, dreaming them
on the rug in the hallway, not able
to watch them calmly, pounced into the luxuriant green...
and plunged into water. I had to flounder back to shore.
But if even the smallest rift had yawned in that pond
at the last moment showing me my bewitching reflection
and stopped me from this. Alas. It wouldn't stop Salmacis
but Narcissus, most likely. And the duck didn't even move,
as if it was wooden, a toy, like the one I had as a child,
watching me indifferently—
the object of desire not feeling its gusts...
As if it was wooden. We did not become one.
A mirror can protect you, remind you that you still are,
even if you become one with desired things.
That time, those duckweeds almost killed me.

February, 2020

About the Translator

A bilingual poet and translator, Jonas Zdanys is the author of fifty-two other books: collections of his own poetry, written in English or in Lithuanian, and volumes of his translations into English of Lithuanian poetry and fiction. He has received a number of prizes, book awards, writing and travel grants, and public recognitions for his own poetry and for his translations. They include Lithuania's Jotvingiai Prize and the National Prize for Literary Translation, major national awards for poetry and for translation given by the Lithuanian Ministry of Culture; two Pushcart Prize nominations; and grants from the Connecticut Commission on the Arts, the National Endowment for the Arts, and the International Research and Exchanges Board/National Endowment for the Humanities. He is a graduate of Yale University and earned a Ph.D. in English from the State University of New York. He has taught at the State University of New York and at Yale University, where he held a number of administrative positions, and served for more than a decade as the state of Connecticut's Chief Academic Officer. He is currently Poet in Residence and Professor Emeritus of English at Sacred Heart University.

www.ingramcontent.com/pod-product-compliance
Lightning Source LLC
Chambersburg PA
CBHW071231070526
44583CB00017B/2137